VOLUNTARY SIMPLICITY

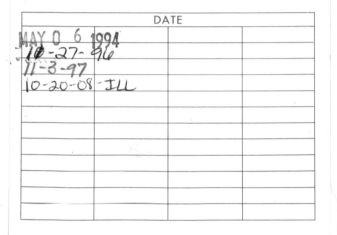

DATE			
MAY 0 6 1994			
10-27-96			
11-3-97			
10-20-08 ILL			

VOLUNTARY SIMPLICITY

TOWARD A WAY OF LIFE
THAT IS OUTWARDLY
SIMPLE, INWARDLY RICH

Revised Edition

DUANE ELGIN

Quill

WILLIAM MORROW

New York

It is the policy of William Morrow and Company, Inc., and its imprints and affiliates, recognizing the importance of preserving what has been written, to print the books we publish on acid-free paper, and we exert our best efforts to that end.

LIBRARY OF CONGRESS CATALOGING-IN-PUBLICATION DATA

Elgin, Duane.
Voluntary simplicity : toward a way of life that is outwardly simple, inwardly rich / Duane Elgin. — Rev. ed.
p.   cm.
Includes bibliographical references and index.
ISBN 0-688-12119-5
1. Simplicity.   I. Title.
BJ1496.E356   1993
179'.9—dc20   92-23740
CIP

Printed in the United States of America

First Quill Edition

1 2 3 4 5 6 7 8 9 10

BOOK DESIGN BY PATRICE FODERO

THIS BOOK IS DEDICATED
WITH LOVE AND APPRECIATION
TO ANN, MARY, CLIFF, BEN, AND MATT

A C K N O W L E D G M E N T S

THERE ARE INNUMERABLE PERSONS WHO HAVE HELPED me along the way—either in the learning that led to the writing of this book or in the writing process itself. I want to acknowledge particularly: my father for his integrity, generosity, and example of patient craftsmanship; my mother for her curiosity, compassion, and zest for life; Daniel Berrigan for teaching me that the way of love does not turn from life; Donald Michael for his enthusiasm for learning with an open mind and open heart; Arnold Mitchell for his collaboration in early research on simpler living as well as his helpful critiques of the early drafts of this book; Ann Niehaus for her abiding love and unconditional support; Ram Dass for his patient reading of early versions of this book and for writing the insightful preface; Frances Vaughan for her encouragement and enthusiasm for this work; Roger Walsh for his friendship, support, and discerning reading of numerous versions of this manuscript; Ronda Davé for her skilled computer analysis of the survey results; and all of the people who responded to the grass-roots survey for bringing a richly human dimension to this work. Finally, I want to acknowledge the assistance of other persons who, in various ways, have helped this work along its path to completion: Barry Bartlett, John Brockman, Joe Dominguez, Andrew Dutter, Sally Furgeson, Paula Hendrick, Bertil Ilhage, Kathryn Reeder, Vicki Robin, Mary Schoonmaker, Peter Schwartz, Peter Teige, Mary Thomas, John White, and Monica Wood.

CONTENTS

Acknowledgments   7

Introduction by Ram Dass   11

LIVING ON THE NEW FRONTIER

*Chapter One: Voluntary Simplicity and the New
Global Challenge*   23

Chapter Two: People Living the Simple Life   57

THE PHILOSOPHY OF SIMPLICITY

Chapter Three: Appreciating Life   113

Chapter Four: Living More Voluntarily   123

Chapter Five: Living More Simply   143

SIMPLICITY AND SOCIAL RENEWAL

Chapter Six: Civilizations in Transition   *163*
Chapter Seven: Civilizational Revitalization   *195*

Appendix: The Simplicity Survey   *219*
Notes   *223*
Suggested Readings   *229*
Index   *233*

Introduction

By Ram Dass

As one who has spent a great deal of time in the East, I've had the chance to view intimately a way of life that, in its simplicity, is very different from the style of living to which we in the West are accustomed.

Even as I write these words, I look out over a gentle valley in the Kumoan Hills at the base of the Himalayas. A river flows through the valley forming now and again man-made tributaries that irrigate the fertile fields. These fields surround the fifty or so thatched or tin-roofed houses and extend in increasingly narrow terraces up the surrounding hillsides.

In several of these fields I watch village men standing on their wooden plows goading on their slow moving water buffalo, who pull the plows, provide the men's families with milk, and help carry their burdens. And amid the green of the hills, in brightly colored saris and nose rings, women cut the high grasses to feed the buffalo and gather the firewood that, along with the dried dung from the buffalo, will provide the fire to cook the grains harvested from the fields and to warm the houses against the winter cold and dry them during the monsoons. A huge haystack passes along the path, seemingly self-propelled, in that the woman on whose head it rests is entirely lost from view.

At a point along the stream there is laughter and talk and the continuous slapping of wet cloth against the rock as the family laundry gets done. And everywhere there are children and dogs, each contributing his or her sound to the voice of the village.

Everywhere there is color: red chili peppers drying on the roofs and saris drying by the river, small green and yellow and blue birds darting among the fruit trees, butterflies and bees tasting their way from one brightly colored flower to another.

I have walked for some five miles from the nearest town to reach this valley. The footpath I have taken is the only means of exit from this village. Along the way I meet farmers carrying squash, burros bearing firewood or supplies, women with brass pots on their heads, schoolchildren, young men dressed in "city clothes." In all of these people I find a quiet, shy dignity, a sense of belonging, a depth of connectedness to these ancient hills.

It all moves as if in slow motion. Time is measured by the sun, the seasons, and the generations. A conch shell sounds from a tiny temple, which houses a deity worshiped in these hills. The stories of this and other deities are recited and sung, and they are honored by flowers and festivals and fasts. They provide a context— vast in its scale of aeons of time, rich with teachings of reincarnation and the morality inherent in the inevitable workings of karma. And it is this context that gives vertical meaning to these villagers' lives with their endless repetition of cycles of birth and death.

This pastoral vision of simplicity has much appeal to those of us in the West for whom life can be full of confusion, distraction, and complexity. In the rush of modern industrial society and in the attempt to maintain our image as successful persons, we feel that we have lost touch with a deeper, more profound part of our being. Yet we feel that we have little time, energy, or cultural support to pursue those areas of life that we know are important. We long for a simpler way of life that allows us to restore some balance to our lives.

Is the vision of simple living provided by this village in the East the answer? Is this an example of a primitive simplicity of the past or of an enlightened simplicity of the future? Gradually I have come to sense that this is not the kind of simplicity that the future holds. Despite its ancient character, the simplicity of the village is still in its "infancy."

Occasionally people show me their new babies and ask me if that peaceful innocence is not just like that of the Buddha. Probably not, I tell them, for within that baby reside all the latent seeds of worldly desire just waiting to sprout as the opportunity arises. On the other hand, the expression on the face of the Buddha, who had seen through the impermanence and suffering associated with such desires, reflects the invulnerability of true freedom.

So it is with this village. Its ecological and peaceful way of living is unconsciously won and thus is vulnerable to the winds of change that fan the latent desires of its people. Even now there is a familiar though jarring note in this sylvan village scene. The sounds of static and that impersonal professional voice of another civilization— the radio announcer—cut through the harmony of sounds as a young man of the village holding a portable radio to his ear comes around a bend. On his arm there is a silver wristwatch, which sparkles in the sun. He looks at me proudly as he passes. And a wave of understanding passes through me. Just behind that radio and wristwatch comes an army of desires that for centuries have gone untested and untasted. As material growth and technological change activate these yearnings, they will transform the hearts, minds, work, and daily life of this village within a generation or two.

Gradually I see that the simplicity of the village has not been consciously chosen as much as it has been unconsciously derived as the product of centuries of unchanging custom and tradition. The East has yet to fully encounter the impact of technological change and material growth. When the East has encountered the latent desires within its people, and the cravings for material goods and social position begin to wear away at the fabric of traditional culture, then it can begin to choose its simplicity consciously. Then the simplicity of the East will be consciously won—voluntarily chosen.

Just as the East still has its time of transition to move through before finding a new place of dynamic equilibrium and conscious balance, so, too, does the West face its own unique time of transition. In the West there are many who have already begun the search for a more conscious balance, a simplicity of living that allows the integration of inner and outer, material and spiritual, masculine and feminine, personal and social, and all of the other polarities that now divide our lives. Since the decade of the 1960s, this search for integration has led many among a whole subculture to explore the learnings of the East. Yet, in attempting to partake deeply of the rich heritage of the East, many, myself included, have tended to diminish the value and relevance of our Western heritage.

My mind flashes back to 1968, when I returned from my first trip to India. Through the eyes of a renunciate I saw comfort and convenience, aesthetics and pleasure, as the sirens seducing me back into the sleep of unconsciousness. So I moved into a cabin in the woods behind my father's house. Each day I bathed out of a pail of cold water, huddled in blankets against the night chill, slept on a thin mat on the floor, and cooked the same food of lentils and rice each day.

Not fifty yards away, in my father's house, there were empty bedrooms, electricity, warm showers, television, and tasty and varied hot meals cooked each day. I would look at that house in the evenings with disdain, which I now suspect was born mainly out of longing. I was running as hard as I could away from Western values even as I was studying in depth the *Bhagavad-Gita,* which says that one must honor one's unique life predicament; one cannot imitate another's. Though in time I surrendered slowly back into that sensual, material ease of the West, I did so with some sense of being a fallen angel, of compromising with a technological society running out of control. I did not know where a skillful balance was to be found. I had been fortunate enough to taste deeply the most generous fruits of two richly developed cultural traditions. Often I felt them churning and pulling within my being as I searched for balance along the vast spectrum of potentials represented by these two perspectives. I felt the dualism within my being. I could not reject the West and embrace the East—both lived within me.

Similarly many among the counterculture of the 1960s withdrew from the emptiness of the industrial Disneyland of worldly delights (where even when you won, you lost) but did not halt their interior journey with an existential renunciation of the West. Many among a whole generation have turned within to the heart and have begun to move beyond intellectual alienation and despair to directly encounter the place where we are all connected, where we are all one. And from that place many have felt drawn to lifestyles in which their contact with their fellow human beings, with nature, and with God could be renewed.

A cycle of learning is being completed. The time of withdrawal is moving into a time of return. The exploration of new ways of living that support new ways of being is a movement that arises from the awakening of compassion—the dawning realization that the fate of the individual is intimately connected with the fate of the whole. It is a movement that arises from the recognition that our task is not only to be here, in the NOW; it is also to now be HERE. And where "here" is must include the fact that we are inhabitants of an aging industrial civilization that is in great need of the insight, perspective, and creativity that the journey to the "East" (to the interior) can bring upon return to the West.

The dualism inherent in our thinking process (which pits materialism against spiritualism, West against East) must be transcended if we are truly to be the inheritors of our evolutionary legacy and the children of a new age. From this perspective the historic Western preoccupation with the intellect and with material consumption need not be viewed as "wrong" or "bad" or necessarily leading to our destruction. Rather, the Western orientation in living may be viewed as a necessary part of an evolutionary stage out of which yet another birth of higher consciousness—as an amalgam of East and West—might subsequently evolve. The Industrial Revolution, then, is part of a larger revolution in living. The West has made its contribution by providing the material basis of life needed to support the widespread unfolding of consciousness. The contribution of the East is the provision of insight into the nature of the conscious unfolding of consciousness. East and West require the learnings of each other if both are to evolve further and realize the potentials that arise in their integration and balance.

Yet what does this mean in worldly terms? What are the practical, down-to-earth expressions of this integration of inner and outer, East and West, personal growth and social transformation? Are there ways of living that express this integrative intention? We must begin by acknowledging there are no "right answers" to these questions. The process of integration of East and West has only just begun to infuse the popular culture in the last few decades. We have only just begun to enter a new age of discovery. A vast new frontier beckons. The "answers" that we seek will be of our own making—they are still in the process of being discovered in our own lives. And yet, for many of us, merely saying this is not enough. We want to see more clearly the larger pattern into which our lives can fit more skillfully. We also want to see more precisely how we might adapt our daily lives to fit harmoniously into this larger pattern of evolution.

What kind of person might assist in the delicate midwifery of revealing to us the nature of the worldly expression of an integration of inner and outer, East and West? Certainly one would be required to have a foot in both the Eastern and the Western perspectives. One must have cultivated in oneself a compassionate consciousness—a balance of head and heart. I think it requires people like E. F. Schumacher, the author of *Small is Beautiful,* who, with compassion and penetrating insight, challenged many of the traditional assumptions of Western industrial societies. And now, with this book on voluntary simplicity, we meet another of these beings, Duane Elgin. People such as Duane are afraid neither to immerse themselves in the problems and potentials of an advanced industrial civilization nor to immerse themselves in the meditative journey. They find in this balancing process neither despair nor Pollyannaish optimism, but an enthusiasm for the dance. They can reveal the complex dynamics of the existing world situation with a wisdom that reflects self-respect, integrity, compassion, and subtle discriminations of the intellect. Such beings look to the future and see through the smoke to the sunlight.

LIVING ON THE

NEW FRONTIER

Chapter One

⚜

VOLUNTARY SIMPLICITY
AND THE NEW GLOBAL
CHALLENGE

AT THE HEART OF THE SIMPLE LIFE IS AN EMPHASIS ON harmonious and purposeful living. Richard Gregg was a student of Gandhi's teaching and, in 1936, he wrote the following about a life of "voluntary simplicity":

> Voluntary simplicity involves both inner and outer condition. It means singleness of purpose, sincerity and honesty within, as well as avoidance of exterior clutter, of many possessions irrelevant to the chief purpose of life. It means an ordering and guiding of our energy and our desires, a partial restraint in some directions in order to secure greater abundance of life in other directions. It involves a deliberate organization of life for a purpose. Of course, as different people have different purposes in life, what is relevant to the purpose of one person might not be relevant to the purpose of another. . . . The degree of

simplification is a matter for each individual to settle for himself.[1]

There is no special virtue to the phrase *voluntary simplicity*—it is merely a label, and a somewhat awkward label at that. Still, it does acknowledge explicitly that simpler living integrates both inner and outer aspects of life into an organic and purposeful whole.

To live more *voluntarily* is to live more deliberately, intentionally, and purposefully—in short, it is to live more consciously. We cannot be deliberate when we are distracted from life. We cannot be intentional when we are not paying attention. We cannot be purposeful when we are not being present. Therefore, to act in a voluntary manner is to be aware of ourselves as we move through life. This requires that we not only pay attention to the actions we take in the outer world, but also that we pay attention to ourselves acting—our inner world. To the extent that we do not notice both inner and outer aspects of our passage through life, then our capacity for voluntary, deliberate, and purposeful action is commensurately diminished.

To live more simply is to live more purposefully and with a minimum of needless distraction. The particular expression of *simplicity* is a personal matter. We each know where our lives are unnecessarily complicated. We are all painfully aware of the clutter and pretense that weigh upon us and make our passage through the world more cumbersome and awkward. To live more simply is to unburden ourselves—to live more lightly, cleanly, aerodynamically. It is to establish a more direct, unpretentious, and unencumbered relationship with all aspects of our lives: the things that we consume, the work that we do, our relationships with others, our connections with nature and the cosmos, and more. Simplicity of living means meeting life face-to-face. It means confronting life clearly, without unnecessary distractions. It means being direct and honest in relationships of all kinds. It means taking life as it is—straight and unadulterated.

When we combine these two ideas for integrating the inner and outer aspects of our lives, we can describe *voluntary simplicity* as a manner of living that is outwardly more simple and inwardly more rich, a way of being in which our most authentic and alive self is brought into direct and conscious contact with living. This way of life is not a static condition to be achieved, but an ever-changing balance that must be continuously and consciously made real. Simplicity in this sense is not simple. To maintain a skillful balance between the inner and outer aspects of our lives is an enormously challenging and continuously changing process. The objective is not dogmatically to live with less, but is a more demanding intention of living with balance in order to find a life of greater purpose, fulfillment, and satisfaction.

MISCONCEPTIONS ABOUT THE SIMPLE LIFE

Some people tend to equate ecological living with a life characterized by poverty, antagonism to progress, rural living, and the denial of beauty. It is important to acknowledge these misconceptions so that we can move beyond them.

Impoverished Living

Although some spiritual traditions have advocated a life of extreme renunciation, it is inaccurate to equate simplicity with poverty. My awakening to the harsh reality of poverty began on my father's farm in Idaho, where I worked with people who lived on the edge of subsistence. I remember one fall harvest when I was about ten years old in the early 1950s. We were harvesting a forty-acre field of lettuce, and a crew of twenty or so migrant laborers arrived to go to work. I still recall a family of three—a father, mother, and a daughter about my age—that drove their old Mercury sedan down the dusty road into our farm. They parked in the field and, with solemn faces, worked through the day doing piece labor—getting paid for the number of crates of lettuce they filled. At the end of the day they received their few dollars of wages as a family, earning roughly sixty-five cents an hour. That evening I returned to the fields with my father to check on the storage of the crates of lettuce and found the family parked at the edge of the field, sitting against the side of their car, and eating an evening meal that consisted of a loaf of white bread, a few slices of lunch meat, and a small jar of mayonnaise. I wondered how they managed to work all day on such a limited meal but asked no questions. When I arrived for work the following morning, they got out of their car where they had slept the night and began working another day. After they had repeated this cycle for three days, the harvest was finished and they left. This was just one of innumerable personal encounters with poverty. Over the next fifteen years I worked in the fields each summer and gradually came to realize that most of these people did not know whether, in another week or month, their needs for food and shelter would be met by their meager salary.

As I worked side by side with these fine people, I saw that poverty has a very human face—one that is very different from "simplicity." Poverty is involuntary and debilitating, whereas simplicity is voluntary and enabling. Poverty is mean and degrading to the human spirit, whereas a life of conscious simplicity can have both a beauty and a functional integrity that elevates the human spirit. Involuntary poverty generates a sense of helplessness, passivity, and despair, whereas purposeful simplicity fosters a sense of personal empowerment, creative engagement, and opportunity.

Historically those choosing a simpler life have sought the golden mean—a creative and aesthetic balance between poverty and excess. Instead of placing primary emphasis on material riches, they have sought to develop, with balance, the invisible wealth of experiential riches.

If the human family sets a goal for itself of achieving a moderate standard of living for everyone, computer projections suggest that the world could reach a sustainable level of economic activity that is roughly "equivalent in material comforts to the average level in Europe in 1990."[2] If we do not delay but act with decision and determination, then humanity need not face a future of poverty and sacrifice. The earth can sustain a moderate and satisfying material standard of living for the entire human family.

Turning Away from Progress

Ecological living does not imply turning away from economic progress; rather it seeks to discover which technologies are most appropriate and helpful in moving toward a sustainable future. Ecological living is not a path of "no growth" but a path of "new growth" that includes both material and spiritual dimensions of life. A simpler way of life is not a retreat from progress; in fact it is essential to the advance of civilizations. After a lifetime of study of the rise and fall of the world's civilizations, historian Arnold Toynbee concluded that the measure of a civilization's growth was not to be found in the conquest of other people or in the possession of land. Rather he described the essence of growth in what he called the *Law of Progressive Simplification.*[3] True growth, he said, is the ability of a society to transfer increasing amounts of energy and attention from the material side of life to the nonmaterial side and thereby to advance its culture, capacity for compassion, sense of community, and strength of democracy. We are now being pushed by necessity to discover freshly the meaning of "true growth" by progressively simplifying the material side of our lives and enriching the nonmaterial side.

Rural Living

In the popular imagination there is a tendency to equate the simple life with Thoreau's cabin in the woods by Walden Pond and to assume that people must live an isolated and rural existence. Interestingly, Thoreau was not a hermit during his stay at Walden Pond. His famous cabin was roughly a mile from the town of Concord, and every day or two he would walk into town. His cabin was so close to a nearby highway that he could smell the pipe smoke of passing travelers. Thoreau wrote that he had "more visitors while I lived in the woods than any other period of my life."[4]

The romanticized image of rural living does not fit the modern reality, as a majority of persons choosing a life of conscious simplicity do not live in the backwoods or rural settings; they live in cities and suburbs. While ecological living brings with it a reverence for nature, this does not require moving to a rural setting. Instead of a "back to the land" movement, it is more accurate to describe this as a "make the most of wherever you are" movement.

Denial of Beauty

The simple life is sometimes viewed as a primitive approach to living that advocates a barren plainness and denies the value of beauty and aesthetics. While the Puritans, for example, were suspicious of the arts, many other advocates of simplicity have seen it as essential for revealing the natural beauty of things. Many who adopt a simpler life would surely agree with Pablo Picasso, who said that "art is the elimination of the unnecessary." The influential architect Frank Lloyd Wright was an advocate of an "organic simplicity" that integrates function with beauty and eliminates the superfluous. In his architecture a building's interior and exterior blend into an organic whole, and the building, in turn, blends harmoniously with the natural environment.[5] Rather than involving a denial of beauty, simplicity liberates the aesthetic sense by freeing things from artificial encumbrances. From a transcendental perspective, simplicity removes the obscuring clutter and discloses the spirit that infuses all things.

It is important to acknowledge these misleading stereotypes because they suggest a life of regress instead of progress. These misconceptions make a simpler life seem impractical and unapproachable and thereby reinforce the feeling that nothing can be done to respond to our critical world situation. To move from denial to action, we need an accurate understanding of the nature of simpler living and its relevance for the modern era.

COMMON EXPRESSIONS OF ECOLOGICAL WAYS OF LIVING

There is no cookbook for defining a life of conscious simplicity. Richard Gregg, for example, was insistent that "simplicity is a relative matter depending on climate, customs, culture, and the character of the individual."[6] Henry David Thoreau was also clear that no simple formula could define the worldly expression of a simpler life. He said, "I would not have anyone adopt my mode of living on my account. . . . I would have each one be very careful to find out and pursue his own way."[7] Nor did Mahatma Gandhi advocate a blind denial of the material side of life. He said, "As long as you derive inner help and comfort from anything, you should keep it. If you were to give it up in a mood of self-sacrifice or out of a stern sense of duty, you would continue to want it back, and that unsatisifed want would make trouble for you. Only give up a thing when you want some other condition so much that the thing no longer has any attraction for you."[8] Because simplicity has as much to do with each person's purpose in living as it does with his or her standard of living, it follows that there is no single, "right and true" way to live more ecologically and compassionately.

Although there is no dogmatic formula for simpler living, there is a general pattern of behaviors and attitudes that is often associated with this approach to living. Those choosing a simpler life:

- Tend to invest the time and energy freed up by simpler living in activities with their partner, children, and friends (walking, making music together, sharing a meal, camping, etc.), or volunteering to help others, or getting involved in civic affairs to improve the life of the community.

- Tend to work on developing the full spectrum of their potentials: physical (running, biking, hiking, etc.), emotional (learning the skills of intimacy and sharing feelings in important relationships), mental (engaging in lifelong learning by reading, taking classes, etc.), and spiritual (learning to move through life with a quiet mind and compassionate heart).

- Tend to feel an intimate connection with the earth and a reverential concern for nature. In knowing that the ecology of the earth is a part of our extended "body," people tend to act in ways that express great care for its well-being.

- Tend to feel a compassionate concern for the world's poor; a simpler life fosters a sense of kinship with people around the world and thus a concern for social justice and equity in the use of the world's resources.

- Tend to lower their overall level of personal consumption—buy less clothing (with more attention to what is functional, durable, aesthetic, and less concern with passing fads, fashions, and seasonal styles), buy less jewelry and other forms of personal ornamentation, buy fewer cosmetic products and observe holidays in a less commercialized manner.

- Tend to alter their patterns of consumption in favor of products that are durable, easy to repair, nonpolluting in their manufacture and use, energy-efficient, functional, and aesthetic.

- Tend to shift their diet away from highly processed foods, meat, and sugar toward foods that are more natural, healthy, simple, and appropriate for sustaining the inhabitants of a small planet.

- Tend to reduce undue clutter and complexity in their personal lives by giving away or selling those possessions that are seldom used and could be used productively by others (clothing, books, furniture, appliances, tools, etc.).

- Tend to use their consumption politically by boycotting goods and services of companies whose actions or policies they consider unethical.

- Tend to recycle metal, glass, and paper and to cut back on consumption of items that are wasteful of nonrenewable resources.

- Tend to pursue a livelihood that directly contributes to the well-being of the world and enables a person to use more fully his or her creative capacities in ways that are fulfilling.

- Tend to develop personal skills that contribute to greater self-reliance and reduce dependence upon experts to handle life's ordinary demands (for example, basic carpentry, plumbing, appliance repair, gardening, crafts, etc.).

- Tend to prefer smaller-scale, more human-sized living and working environments that foster a sense of community, face-to-face contact, and mutual caring.

- Tend to alter male-female roles in favor of non-sexist patterns of relationship.

- Tend to appreciate the simplicity of nonverbal forms of communication—the eloquence of silence, hugging and touching, the language of the eyes.

- Tend to participate in holistic health-care practices that emphasize preventive medicine and the healing powers of the body when assisted by the mind.

- Tend to involve themselves with compassionate causes, such as protecting rain forests and saving animals from extinction, and tend to use nonviolent means in their efforts.

- Tend to change transportation modes in favor of public transit, car pooling, smaller and more fuel-efficient autos, living closer to work, riding a bike, and walking.

Because there is a tendency to emphasize the external changes that characterize simpler living, it is important to reiterate that this approach to life is intended to integrate both inner and outer aspects of existence into a satisfying and purposeful whole.

Maintaining Ourselves and Surpassing Ourselves

An ecological approach to living invites us to continuously balance two aspects of life—maintaining ourselves (creating a workable existence) and surpassing ourselves (creating a meaningful existence). A statement by the philosopher and feminist Simone de Beauvoir helps clarify this: "Life is occupied in both perpetuating itself and in surpassing itself; if all it does is maintain itself, then living is only not dying." On the one hand, if we seek *only* to maintain ourselves, then no matter how grand our style of living might be, we are doing little more than "only not dying." On the other hand, if we strive *only* for a meaningful existence without securing the material foundation that supports our lives, then our physical existence is in jeopardy and the opportunity to surpass ourselves becomes little more than a utopian dream. Although many of the expressions of a simpler life listed above emphasize actions that promote a more sustainable existence, this should not distract us from the importance of the surpassing or inner dimensions of a life of conscious simplicity.

The many expressions of simpler living, both inner and outer, indicate that this is much more than a superficial change in the *style* of life. A "style" change refers generally to an exterior change, such as a new fad or fashion. Simplicity goes far deeper and involves a change in our *way* of life. Ecological living is a sophisticated response to the demands of deteriorating industrial civilizations. Table 1 shows the contrasts between the worldview of the industrial era and that of the emerging ecological era. Simpler ways of living in the ecological era will result in changes as great as the transition from the agrarian era to the industrial era. In an interdependent, ecologically conscious world every aspect of life will be touched and changed: consumption levels and patterns, living and working environments, political attitudes and processes, international ethics and relations, the uses of mass media, education, and many more.

THE PUSH OF NECESSITY AND THE PULL OF OPPORTUNITY

Two compelling reasons exist for choosing more ecological approaches to living: the push of necessity and the pull of opportunity. The combined impact of the various *pushes of necessity* are staggering to contemplate. Here is an overview of our predicament:

- In 1930 the world had 2 billion people, in 1975 roughly 4 billion people, by the year 2000 the population is expected to exceed 6 billion people, and 2025 the world's population will approach 9 billion people. The vast majority of the increase in human numbers is occurring in the less-developed nations. Because the world's ecosystem is already under

TABLE 1: CONTRASTS IN WORLDVIEW BETWEEN THE INDUSTRIAL ERA AND THE ECOLOGICAL ERA

Industrial-Era View	*Ecological-Era View*
The goal in life is material progress.	The goal in life is to co-evolve both the material and spiritual aspects with harmony and balance.
Emphasis on conspicuous consumption—the "good life" is dependent upon having enough money to buy access to life's pleasures and to avoid life's discomforts.	Emphasis on conservation and frugality—using only as much as is needed; a satisfying life emerges with balanced development in cooperation with others.
Identity is defined by material possessions and social position.	Identity is revealed through our loving and creative participation in life.
The individual is defined by his or her body and is ultimately separate and alone.	The individual is both unique and an inseparable part of the larger universe; identity is not limited to our physical existence.
The universe is viewed as material and largely lifeless; it is natural that we who are living exploit the lifeless universe for our ends.	The universe is a living organism that is infused with a subtle life-force; it is important to act in ways that honor the preciousness and dignity of all life.

Industrial-Era View	Ecological-Era View
Emphasis on self-serving behavior (get as much for myself as I can while giving no more than is required in return).	Emphasis on life-serving behavior (give as much of myself to life as I am able and ask in return no more than I require).
Cutthroat competition prevails; compete against others and strive to "make a killing."	Fair competition prevails; cooperate with others and work to earn a living.
The mass media are dominated by commercial interests and are used aggressively to promote a high-consumption culture.	The mass media are used to promote a balanced diet of information and messages, including the importance of ecological approaches to living.
Nations adopt a "lifeboat ethic" in global relations.	Nations adopt a "spaceship Earth ethic" in global relations.
The welfare of the whole is left to the workings of the free market and/or government bureaucracies.	Each person takes responsibility for the well-being of the world.
Emphasis on personal autonomy and mobility.	Emphasis on connectedness and community.

great stress, as these new billions of persons seek a decent standard of living, the global ecology could easily be strained beyond the breaking point, producing a calamity of unprecedented proportions.

- The gap between rich and poor nations is already a chasm and is growing wider rapidly. The average person in the richest one-fifth of the world's countries earned $15,000 in 1990, whereas the average person in the poorest one-fifth of the world's countries earned $250. This sixty-fold differential between the rich and poor is double what it was in 1960.[9]

- More than a thousand million people (1.2 billion) now live in absolute poverty—"a condition of life so limited by malnutrition, illiteracy, disease, squalid surroundings, high infant mortality and low life expectancy as to be beneath any reasonable definition of human decency."[10]

- Global warming will likely alter patterns of rainfall and disrupt food production, flood enormous areas of low-lying lands, displace millions of people, destroy fragile ecosystems, and alter patterns of disease in unpredictable ways.[11]

- Tropical rain forests are being cut down at an alarming rate, contributing to global warming and destroying precious ecosystems that required millions of years to evolve (and that contain a treasury of undiscovered pharmaceuticals).

- Cheaply available supplies of oil are being depleted rapidly and, within a generation, the world will be deprived of an energy source basic to our current form of high-intensity agriculture.

- Toxic wastes are being poured into the environment, and pollution-induced outbreaks of cancer and genetic damage may reach massive proportions.

- Overfishing and pollution of the world's oceans have led to a leveling off in annual fish catch at the same time that the demand for food from the world's oceans is increasing.

- The ozone layer is thinning over populated regions of both the Southern and the Northern Hemispheres and threatens to cause skin cancer and cataracts in humans and unknown damage to the rest of the food chain.

- Thousands of plant and animal species are becoming extinct each year, representing the greatest loss of life on the planet since the massive extinction of dinosaurs and other animal and plant life roughly 65 million years ago.

- Acid rains from coal burning and sulfur-producing industrial processes are damaging forests, farmland, and freshwater streams.

These are not isolated problems; instead they comprise a tightly intertwined system of problems that require us to develop new approaches to living if we are to live sustainably. To live *sustainably,* we must live efficiently—not misdirecting or squandering the earth's precious resources. To live *efficiently,* we must live peacefully, for military expenditures represent an enormous diversion of resources from meeting basic human needs. To live *peacefully,* we must live with a reasonable degree of *equity,* or fairness, for it is unrealistic to think that, in a communications-rich world, a billion or more persons will accept living in absolute poverty while another billion live in conspicuous excess. Only with greater fairness in the consumption of the world's resources can we live peacefully, and thereby live sustainably, as a human family. Without a revolution in fairness, the world will find itself in chronic conflict over dwindling resources, and this in turn will make it impossible to achieve the level of cooperation necessary to solve problems such as pollution and overpopulation.

The United Nations *Human Development Report* of 1992 said, "In a world of 5 billion people, we discovered that the top billion people hold 83 percent of the world's wealth, while the bottom billion have only 1.4 percent."[12] We cannot expect to live in a peaceful world with such enormous disparities between the rich and the poor. The prosperity of the technologically interdependent, wealthy nations is vulnerable to disruption by terrorism by those who have nothing left to lose and no hope for the future. *Only with greater equity can we expect to live peacefully, and only with greater harmony can we expect to live sustainably.*

If the world is profoundly divided materially, there is very little hope that it can be united socially, psychologically, and spiritually. Therefore if we intend to live together peacefully as members of a single, human family, then each individual has a right to a reasonable share of the world's resources. Each person has a right to expect a fair share of the world's wealth sufficient to support a "decent" standard of living—one that provides enough food, shelter, education, and health care to enable people to realize their potentials as productive and respected members of the family of humanity. This does not mean that the world should adopt a single manner and standard of living; rather, it means that each person needs to feel part of the global family and, within a reasonable range of differences, valued and supported in realizing his or her unique human potentials.

With sustainability we can expand our experiential riches of culture, compassion, community, and self-determination. With a growing abundance of experiential riches the entire process of living will be encouraged, and a self-reinforcing spiral of development will unfold. Therefore, reinforcing the powerful push of necessity is the *pull of opportunity*—the potential of the simple life to yield a more satisfying and soulful existence. Many persons in developed nations find life to be psychologically and spiritually hollow—living in massive urban environments of alienating scale and complexity, divorced from the natural environment, and working in

jobs that are unsatisfying. Many yearn for a more authentic approach to living, one that provides a fulfilling
relationship with oneself, with others, with the earth,
and with the universe. *Time* magazine and CNN television conducted a survey of Americans for *Time*'s April
8, 1991, cover story entitled "The Simple Life." The
results are striking:

- Sixty-nine percent of the people surveyed said
  they would like to "slow down and live a more
  relaxed life," in contrast to only 19 percent who
  said they would like to "live a more exciting,
  faster-paced life."

- Sixty-one percent agreed that "earning a living
  today requires so much effort that it's difficult to
  find time to enjoy life."

- When asked about their priorities, 89 percent said
  it was more important these days to spend time
  with their families.

- Only 13 percent saw importance in keeping up
  with fashion trends, and just 7 percent thought
  it was worth bothering to shop for status-symbol
  products.

Another survey reported in a 1989 article in *Fortune*
magazine entitled "Is Greed Dead?" found that 75 percent of working Americans between the ages of twenty-

five and forty-nine would like "to see our country return to a simpler lifestyle, with less emphasis on material success."[13] Only 10 percent of those polled thought that "earning a lot of money" was an indicator of success. These polls reveal that a large fraction of the American public has experienced the limited rewards from the material riches of a consumer society and is looking for the experiential riches that can be found, for example, in satisfying relationships, living in harmony with nature, and being of service to the world.

The combination of the push of necessity and the pull of opportunity creates an entirely new situation for humanity. On the one hand, a life of creative simplicity frees energy for the soulful work of spiritual discovery and loving service—tasks that all of the world's wisdom traditions say we should give our highest priority. On the other hand, a simpler way of life also responds to the urgent needs for moderating our use of the world's nonrenewable resources and minimizing the damaging impact of environmental pollution. Working in concert, these pushes and pulls are creating an immensely powerful dynamic for transforming our ways of living, working, relating, and thinking.

HISTORICAL ROOTS OF SIMPLICITY

While simpler living has unprecedented relevance for coping with the current ecological crisis, it has deep roots in human experience. Although these historical roots are far too extensive to examine in depth, a brief review helps to reveal the breadth and richness of this approach to living.[14]

Christian Views

Jesus embodied a life of compassionate simplicity. He taught by work and example that we should not make the acquisition of material possessions our primary aim; instead we should develop our capacity for loving participation in life. The Bible speaks frequently about the need to find a balance between the material and the spiritual side of life; for example:

- "Give me neither poverty nor wealth." (Proverbs 30:8)
- "Do not store up for yourselves treasure on earth, where it grows rusty and moth-eaten, and thieves break in to steal it. Store up treasure in heaven. . . . For wherever your treasure is, there will your heart be also." (Matthew 6:19–21)
- "Therefore I tell you, do not be anxious about

> your life, what you shall eat or what you shall
> drink, nor about your body, what you shall put
> on. Is not life more than food, and the body more
> than clothing?" (Matthew 6:25)

- "If a man has enough to live on, and yet when
  he sees his brother in need shuts up his heart
  against him, how can it be said that the divine
  love dwells in him?" (John 3:17)

A common basis for living simply can be found in
all the world's spiritual traditions and is expressed in
the "golden rule"—the compassionate admonition that
we should treat others as we would want ourselves to
be treated. The theme of sharing and economic justice
seems particularly strong in the Christian tradition. Basil
the Great, bishop of Caesarea, stated around A.D. 365:
"When someone steals a man's clothes we call him a
thief. Should we not give the same name to one who
could clothe the naked and does not? The bread in your
cupboard belongs to the hungry man; the coat hanging
unused in your closet belongs to the man who needs it;
the shoes rotting in your closet belong to the man who
has not shoes; the money which you hoard up belongs
to the poor."[15] In the modern era this implies that if
people in developed nations consume more than their
fair share of the world's resources, then they are taking
food, clothing, and other essentials from those who are
in great need.

A contemporary expression of simplicity in the
Christian tradition is found in the "Shakertown Pledge,"
a statement developed in 1973 by a diverse group of
Christians in an effort to describe a lifestyle appropriate
to the new realities of the world.[16] Two key commitments
give a feeling for this pledge: "I commit myself to lead
an ecologically sound life," and "I commit myself to
lead a life of creative simplicity and to share my personal
wealth with the world's poor." These commitments are
not meant to produce a pinched and miserly existence;
instead they are intended to encourage an aesthetic simplicity that enhances personal freedom and fulfillment
while promoting a just manner of living relative to the
needs of the world.

Eastern Views

Eastern spiritual traditions such as Buddhism,
Hinduism and Taoism have also encouraged a life of
material moderation and spiritual abundance. From the
Taoist tradition we have this saying from Lao-tzu: "He
who knows he has enough is rich."[17] From the Hindu
tradition we have these thoughts from Mahatma Gandhi,
the spiritual and political leader who was instrumental
in gaining India's independence: "Civilization, in the real
sense of the term, consists not in the multiplication, but
in the deliberate and voluntary reduction of wants. This

alone promotes real happiness and contentment."[18] Gandhi felt the moderation of our wants increases our capacity to be of service to others and, in being of loving service to others, true civilization emerges.

Perhaps the most developed expression of a middle way between material excess and deprivation comes from the Buddhist tradition. While Buddhism recognizes that basic material needs must be met in order to realize our potentials, it does not consider our material welfare as an end in itself; rather, it is a means to the end of awakening to our deeper nature as spiritual beings. Self-control and a simple life are valued highly, as is the practice of charity and generosity without attachment to one's wealth or property.[19] A modern expression of this view is given by the monk Sulak Sivaraksa, who describes the necessity for a more compassionate and simple way of living: "We can only save ourselves when all humanity recognizes that every problem on earth is our own personal problem and our personal responsibility. . . . Unless the rich change their lifestyle considerably, there is no hope of solving [the problem of famine in the world]."[20]

E. F. Schumacher, author of the classic book *Small Is Beautiful,* described Buddhism as a middle path that emphasizes simplicity and nonviolence.[21] Applying the middle way to economics, Schumacher described a Buddhist economy as one that provides an adequate range of material goods and whose production processes are in harmony with both the environment and available resources. The middle way of Buddhist economics moves between mindless materialism, on the one hand, and needless poverty, on the other. The result is a balanced approach to living that harmonizes both inner and outer development.

Early Greek Views

Plato and Aristotle recognized the importance of the "golden mean" or a middle path through life characterized by neither excess nor deficit, but by sufficiency. Like many spiritual traditions, they did not view the material world as primary but as instrumental—as serving our learning about the more expansive world of thought and spirit. Plato's teacher, Socrates, also advocated a golden mean between wealth and poverty. Aristotle favored a balanced life that involved moderation on the material side and exertion on the intellectual side. He said that "temperance and courage" were destroyed by either excess or deficiency and could only be preserved by following the golden mean.[22]

Puritan Views

Paradoxically, although the United States is the world's most blatantly consumerist nation, the simple life has strong roots in American history. The early Puritan settlers brought to America their "puritan ethic," which stressed hard work, temperate living, participation in the life of the community, and a steadfast devotion to things spiritual. Puritans also stressed the golden mean by saying we should not desire more material things than we can use effectively. It is from the New England Puritans that we get the adage, Use it up, wear it out, make do, or do without. Although the Puritan tradition tended to be hierarchical, elitist, and authoritarian, it also had a compassionate side that encouraged people to use their excess wealth to help the deserving poor. Puritans were not opposed to prosperity itself, but to the greed and selfishness that seemed to accompany excessive abundance.

Quaker Views

The Quakers also had a strong influence on the American character, particularly with their belief that material simplicity was an important aid in evolving toward spiritual perfection. Unlike the Puritans, their strong sense of equality among people fostered religious tolerance. Quakers emphasized the virtues of hard work at one's calling, sobriety, and frugality. Although they thought it only natural for one to enjoy the fruits of their labor, they also recognized that our stay on earth is brief and that people should place much of their love and attention on things eternal.

Transcendentalist Views

Transcendentalist views flourished in the early to mid-1800s in America and are best exemplified by the lives and writing of Ralph Waldo Emerson and Henry David Thoreau. The Transcendentalists believed that a spiritual presence infuses the world and, by living simply, we can more easily encounter this miraculous and vital Life-force. For Emerson the Transcendental path began with self-discovery and then led to "an organic synthesis of that self with the natural world surrounding it."[23] The Transcendentalists had a reverential attitude toward nature and saw the natural world as the doorway to the divine. Nature was seen as the most fitting place for contemplation and receiving spiritual inspiration. By communing with nature, Emerson felt that people could become "part and parcel with God," thereby realizing the ultimate simplicity of oneness with the divine. Thoreau also viewed simplicity as a means to a higher end. Although he felt that a person "is rich in proportion to the number of things which he can afford to let alone," he was not particularly concerned with the specific manner in which someone lived a simpler life. Instead he was most interested in the rich inner life that could be gained through undistracted contemplation. For both Emerson and Thoreau, simplicity had more to do with one's intentions than with one's particular possessions.

This brief overview illustrates the long and rich tradition of simplicity of living in human experience. Historian of the simple life David Shi describes the common denominator among the various approaches to simpler living as the understanding that the making of money and the accumulation of things should not smother the purity of the soul, the life of the mind, the cohesion of the family, or the good of the society.[24] Clearly the simple life is not a new social invention—its value has long been recognized. What is new is the urgent need to respond to the radically changed material and ecological circumstances in which humanity finds itself in the modern world.

THE RESPONSIBILITY FOR CHANGE

Unless dramatic changes are made in the manner of living and consuming in industrialized nations, we will soon produce a world of monumental destruction, suffering, conflict, and despair. Within this generation we must begin a sweeping reinvention of our ways of living or invite the collapse of our biosphere and allow global civilization to veer off into a long detour and dark age.

Because we face a crisis in the interconnected global system, changes at every level are needed. At the personal level we need a magnified global awareness and simpler ways of living. At the neighborhood level we need new types of communities for sustainable living. At the national level we need to adopt new policies with regard to energy, environment, education, media, and many more. At the global level we need new partnerships among nations. Although changes are necessary at every level, the foundation upon which success can be built is the individual and the family. It is empowering to know that each person can make a difference by taking responsibility for changes in his or her immediate life.

Just as we tend to wait for our problems to solve themselves, so, too, do we tend to wait for our traditional institutions and leaders to provide us with guidance as to what we should do. Yet our leaders are bogged down, trying to cope with our faltering institutions. They are so enmeshed in crisis management that they have little time to exercise genuinely creative leadership. We may keep waiting for someone else, but a key message of this book is that there is no one else. You are it. We are it. Each of us is responsible. It is we who, one by one, must take charge of our lives. It is we who, one by one, must act to restore the balance. We are the ones who are responsible for making it through this time of sweeping change as we work to build a sustainable future for the planet.

*   *   *

Before proceeding it may be helpful to describe briefly the remainder of the book. The next section draws upon the real-life experiences of people in order to provide a realistic description of simpler living. The following section examines the philosophy of simplicity and considers both the inner and the outer aspects of an ecological approach to living. The final section considers the challenges facing aging industrial civilizations and how ecological ways of living could become a powerful force for revitalization.

Chapter Two

⚜

PEOPLE LIVING THE

SIMPLE LIFE

IN THE LAST SEVERAL DECADES, A GROWING NUMBER OF people have been exploring a simpler way of life. Without major media coverage to mark its progress, the growth in simpler ways of living has emerged largely unnoticed in many developed nations. Quietly and without fanfare people have been developing ways of living that touch the world more lightly and compassionately; for example:

- A city dweller plants an intensive garden and volunteers time to work with the homeless.
- A busy executive begins meditating to reduce stress and, as a result, he finds more satisfaction in the flow of living and is less interested in the old business game of acquiring power, status, and money.

- A suburban family insulates its home, buys a fuel-efficient car, begins to recycle glass, cans, and paper and shifts its diet away from meat and highly processed foods.

- A lawyer learns carpentry as an alternative profession, shops for clothes in secondhand stores, and buys used books.

Although these may seem like inconsequential changes in response to the immense challenges facing our world, they are of great significance. The character of a whole society is the cumulative result of the countless small actions, day in and day out, of millions of persons. Small changes that may seem unimportant in isolation are of transformative significance when adopted by an entire society. Because increasing numbers of people are experimenting with more ecological ways of living, there is a realistic possibility that we can build a sustainable future.

In this chapter we will see, through the living example of several hundred persons from all walks of life, that there are workable and satisfying responses to the urgent challenges we now face. The power of living examples to teach was brought home to me a number of years ago while attending a conference with a number of leading thinkers who were exploring the concept of a transforming society. Although the meetings were of great interest and many grand pronouncements were made concerning the need for social change, I now remember none of what was said. However, I do remember having lunch with Elise Boulding—a devout Quaker, feminist, sociologist, and compassionate advocate of the need for nonviolent, though fundamental, social change. At the end of the first morning's discussion we emerged from conference rooms to encounter an enormous buffet heaped with fruits, cheeses, salads, meats, breads, and more. Having worked up a considerable appetite, I filled my plate and sat down next to Elise. She had, without comment or display, selected for her lunch an apple, a piece of cheese, and a slice of bread. I was surprised that she had chosen such a modest lunch when such a bountiful offering was available. I asked Elise how she felt, and though she reassured me that she was feeling fine, I was still puzzled. I persisted and asked why she had taken such a small helping. In a few quiet sentences she explained that she did not want to eat what others in the world could not have as well. In this seemingly small incident I encountered a practical expression of the compassionate awareness that our individual well-being is inseparable from the well-being of other members of the human family. It is interesting and instructive that I don't remember any of the ideas from that conference, but I do recall what Elise had for lunch that day years ago—and why. I saw that it is the example of each person's life, much more than his or her words, that speaks with power. Even the smallest action done with a loving appreciation of life can touch other human beings in profound ways. I also saw that we each carry within ourselves the capacity for directly sensing appropriate action as we make our way through this complex and often confusing world.

THE SIMPLICITY SURVEY

While working as a social scientist and "futurist" at a major think tank (SRI International) in 1977, I coauthored an article on voluntary simplicity with a colleague, Arnold Mitchell. This article was published in the *Co-Evolution Quarterly*—a journal whose readership included many persons who have adopted ecological ways of living. We included a questionnaire with this article (shown in the appendix) that asked people to describe their experiences for us. In the eighteen months after this article was published, more than 420 questionnaires and over 200 letters (totaling more than 1,000 pages) were received. Nearly every letter offered a revealing journey into the lives of an individual or family. Many letters were inspiring and empowering. Some were light and humorous. A few were despairing. I read each of the letters at least four times and was impressed with the compassion, humor, and courage of these individuals and families. Here is the background of these respondents:

- People from all walks of life responded—lawyers, teachers, social workers, students, government bureaucrats, firemen, carpenters, factory workers, retired couples, white-collar workers, and more.

- Responses were received from forty-two states in the United States as well as from several European countries, Canada, and Australia.

- A broad spectrum of ages was represented—from seventeen to sixty-seven. The average age was roughly thirty, and 75 percent were under the age of thirty-five.

- Nearly all respondents were white.

- Overall income levels tended to be somewhat lower than that of the general U.S. population.

- Most were highly educated—roughly 70 percent had completed college.

- A majority (56 percent) lived in cities and suburbs, 13 percent lived in smaller towns, and 32 percent lived in rural areas.

- Most grew up in relatively affluent homes (71 percent had a middle-class economic background and 22 percent had an upper-class economic background).

• The average respondent had been choosing a simpler way of life for six years.

This background information reveals a number of important insights. First, the wide geographic distribution of respondents indicates this is not a regional phenomenon but includes persons throughout the United States and other Western nations. Second, the fact that a majority of persons were living in urban settings indicates this is not a predominantly "back to the land" movement. Third, the fact that virtually all respondents were white and had childhood backgrounds of relative affluence indicates that the early adopters, or innovators, are not likely to come from those groups who grew up with poverty and discrimination. Fourth, the fact that respondents earned a moderately wide range of income suggests that, within limits, the manner in which one's income is used is as important as the size of income earned. Fifth, the relatively high levels of education of this forerunner group indicates they are not unskilled and poorly educated dropouts from society but, instead, are well-educated and skilled persons who are searching for ways of living and working that are more sustainable and satisfying. Sixth, the fact that the average length of time persons had been involved with this way of living was six years makes it clear that this is not a short-lived, lifestyle fad.

I have drawn a representative sampling of comments

concerning a broad range of topics from over one hundred of the more than two hundred letters received. In order to ensure the privacy of these individuals and still reveal some of the flavor of their lives, each quotation is identified by the person's sex, age, marital status, degree of urbanization of residence, and geographic locale.

WHAT IS VOLUNTARY SIMPLICITY?

To begin, let's see how this group (which practices what it preaches) defines this way of life for themselves.

Voluntary simplicity has more to do with the state of mind than a person's physical surroundings and possessions.
(woman, twenty-three, single, small town, East)

Simplicity meant I fit easier into the more ecological patterns, hence was more flexible, more adaptable, and ultimately more aware of the natural spiritual path before me; less nonsense in the way.
(man, thirty, single, small town, West)

As my spiritual growth expanded and developed, voluntary simplicity was a natural outgrowth. I came to realize the cost of material accumulation was too high and offered fewer and fewer real rewards, psychological and spiritual.
(man, twenty-six, single, small town, South)

I don't think of it as voluntary simplicity. I am simply going through a process of self-knowledge and self-realization, attempting to better the world for myself, my children, my grandchildren, and so on.

(woman, thirty-eight, married, suburb, East)

To me, voluntary simplicity means integration and awareness in my life.

(woman, twenty-seven, single, city, South)

In realizing true identity (a continuing process), voluntary simplicity naturally follows.

(man, age unspecified, living together, small town, West)

Ecological consciousness is a corollary of human consciousness. If you do not respect the human rights of other people, you cannot respect the earth. The desires for material simplicity and a human-scale environment are results of an ecological consciousness.

(man, twenty-six, single, small town, West)

I can't call us living simply but rather living creatively and openly.

(man, thirty-one, married, rural, West)

Voluntary simplicity is not poverty, but searching for a new definition of quality—and buying only what is productively used.

(man, twenty-eight, married, rural, West)

> We laugh that we are considered a "poverty" family, as
> we consider our lives to be rich and full and completely
> rewarding—we are living in harmony with everything. I
> know for myself the source of "richness" or "poverty"
> comes from within me.
>
> *(woman, forty-one, married, rural, West)*

While each person had their own, unique description
of the simple life, a common theme was a concern for
the psychological and spiritual aspects of living. Still,
the diversity of definitions was important, as many said
they were wary of rigid views that would be dogmatically
applied and result in a self-righteous, "simpler-than-
thou" attitude.

Another concern expressed in the letters was that
simpler living would not be seen as a fundamental
change in the *way* of life and, instead, would be tri-
vialized by the mass media and portrayed as only a faddish and superficial change in outward *style* of life. Here
are two illustrative comments:

> This is a country of media hype, and [simple living] is
> good copy. The media is likely to pick up on it . . . and
> create a movement. I hope they won't. The changes we're
> talking about are fundamental and take lots of time. . . . If
> it is made into a movement, it could burn itself out. I hope

it spreads slowly. This way the changes will be more pervasive. Voluntary simplicity is the kind of thing that people need to discover for themselves.

(man, twenty-seven, single, rural, Midwest)

Make a movement out of a spontaneous tendency like voluntary simplicity and the best aspects of it (and the individuals) will elude you.

(woman, thirty, living together, rural, West)

Many of the persons experimenting with simpler ways of living said they did not view themselves as part of a conscious social movement. Instead they were acting on their own initiative to bring their lives in greater harmony with the needs and realities of the world.

WHY CHOOSE SIMPLICITY?

Why would an individual or couple adopt a way of life that is more materially frugal, ecologically oriented, inner directed, and in other ways removed from the traditional ways of life of Western society? Here is a sampling of the reasons given:

I believe in the imminent need for the skills and resources I am developing now. I am not sure how it will come about, whether economic collapse, fuel exhaustion, or natural disaster, but whichever it is, I (and my family) will need all of whatever self-sufficiency I or we can develop.

(man, twenty-nine, married, rural, West)

I believe voluntary simplicity is more compassionate and conducive to personal and spiritual growth. I live this way because I am appalled that half the planet lives in dire poverty while we overconsume. And people think they are "Christian." I think it is "spiritual" to make sure that everyone has adequate food, shelter, and clothing and to take care of the planet.

(woman, twenty-five, married, big city, Midwest)

I sincerely believe that voluntary simplicity is essential to the solution of global problems of environmental pollution, resource scarcity, socioeconomic inequities and existential/spiritual problems of alienation, anxiety, and lack of meaningful lifestyles.

(man, thirty-two, married, suburb, South)

I have less and less to blame on other people. I am more self-reliant. I can both revel in the independence and be frustrated by my shortcomings—but I get to learn from my own mistakes. Each step is progress in independence; freedom is the goal.

(man, twenty-six, married, small town, East)

The main motivation for me is inner spiritual growth and to give my children an idea of the truly valuable and higher things in this world.

   (woman, thirty-eight, single, small town, East)

I feel more voluntary about my pleasures and pains than the average American who has his needs dictated by Madison Ave. (my projection of course). I feel sustained, excited, and constantly growing in my spiritual and intellectual pursuits.

   (woman, thirty, living together, rural, West)

Why simplicity? I see it as the only moral, economic, rational, humanistic goal. Besides, it's fun.

   (man, twenty-three, single, small city, Midwest)

It was the injustice and not the lack of luxury during the Great Depression that disturbed me. I took up this way of life when I was seventeen. I remember choosing this simplicity—not poverty—because: (1) it seemed more just in the face of deprivation—better distribution of goods; (2) more honest—why take or have more than one needs? (3) much freer—why burden oneself with getting and caring for just "things" when time and energy could be spent in so many other more interesting and higher pursuits? (4) but I wanted a simplicity that would include beauty and creativity—art, music, literature, an aesthetic environment—but simply.

   (woman, sixty, married, suburb, West)

Our interest in simpler living dates to overseas tours with the U.S. embassy in underdeveloped nations—we know firsthand what the problems are.

(woman, sixty-one, married, suburb, East)

I felt the values involved in consumerism to be false, useless, and destructive. I prefer to appear as I am. People are complex enough to understand without excess trappings. I was also influenced by the values of the feminist and ecological movements.

(woman, twenty-five, married, suburb, South)

Increasing my self-sufficiency seemed the only honest way to effectively make my feelings, actions, and life congruent.

(man, twenty-seven, married, rural, East)

It is a highly rewarding way to live. It forces you into a relationship with a basic reality. . . . It also forces you to deal with some direct anxieties and rely on and be thankful to a benevolent deity. It succinctly points out your frailty and clearly delineates your dependencies. It also reinforces your strength and independence.

(married couple, thirty-seven and thirty-two, rural, West)

I wanted to remove my children from the superficial, competitive (East Coast) value system. Wanted a family venture to draw us closer and a community that was stable. Also wanted to provide the children with a learning experience that exposes them to alternatives to the "rat race" system, plus I wanted out from the typical pressures of maintaining material acquisitions that were meaningless to me.

(woman, thirty-six, single, rural, West)

Overall the most common reasons given for choosing to live more lightly were to find a more skillful balance between one's inner experience and its outer expression in work, consumption, relationships, and community; to search for a workable and meaningful alternative to the emptiness of a society obsessed with material consumption and display; to provide one's children with more humane value systems and life experiences that are appropriate to the emerging world they will have to live in; to find a much higher degree of independence and self-determination in a mass society of alienating scale and complexity; to establish more cooperative and caring relationships; to acknowledge and, in small but personally meaningful ways, begin to reduce the vast inequities between the rich and the poor around the world; to cope in a personal manner with environmental pollution and resource scarcity; to foster nonsexist ways of relating; to develop the personal skills and know-how to survive a time of severe economic and social disruption; and to create the personal circumstances of life in which one's feelings, thoughts, and actions can come into alignment.

THE PATH TO ECOLOGICAL LIVING

What is the pathway from the industrial-era way of life to voluntary simplicity? Is this way of life chosen abruptly or does it evolve gradually? Here is a sample of comments:

We are moving toward a life of greater simplicity from within, and the external changes are following—perhaps more slowly. We are seeking quality of life—and a path with heart.

(woman, age unspecified, married, suburb, West)

Voluntary simplicity must evolve over a lifetime according to the needs of an individual. . . . The person must grow and be open to new ideas—not jump on a bandwagon, but thoughtfully consider ideas and see how they relate to oneself.

(woman, twenty-one, single, small city, Midwest)

[Voluntary simplicity is] a thorough lifestyle that only works through full commitment and takes many years to grow into.

(man, twenty-nine, married, small town, West)

Simplicity began unfolding in my life as a process. It was an inarticulate but seemingly sensible response to emerging situations—and one response after another began to form a pattern, which you identify as voluntary simplicity. For me simplicity was the result of a growing awareness plus a sense of social responsibility.

(man, thirty-one, married, small town, West)

To me, voluntary simplicity as a lifestyle is not something you take up in one moment, but occurs over a period of time due to: (1) consciousness raising; (2) peer group support; (3) background; (4) inner-growth interest; and many other factors. My wholehearted commitment to a certain spiritual path finds outer expression in a simple, gentle, humane lifestyle.

(woman, twenty-eight, single, suburb, West)

It wasn't a slam-bang, bolt-from-the-blue, overnight change. I'm still growing and learning. The most important goal I have is inner development with a good blend of living with the here and now on this planet.

(man, twenty-five, married, small town, East)

I consciously started to live simply when I started to become conscious. . . . Living simply is in the flow of things for me.

(man, thirty, married, rural, East)

My ideas and my practice of voluntary simplicity have been and I hope will continue to be a gradual process of evolution and growth. From early adolescence on I tended to prefer simplicity.

(woman, twenty-one, single, small city, Midwest)

Various flirtations with yoga, meditation, drugs, and radical politics gave me exposure to, and some personal experience with, "inner growth" possibilities. I began living my life freely, following no preconceived roles, and gradually discovered my overriding interest in quality: the environment, life, the universe.

(man, twenty-nine, married, small town, East)

I became interested in simplicity . . . primarily because of ecological concerns. However, since then my interest has become concentrated more on metaphysics, self-realization, and so on, with the same end results.

(woman, thirty-eight, married, big city, Midwest)

Voluntary simplicity is an individual thing. . . . It has to be something that springs from the heart because it was always there, not something you can be talked in to by persuasive people, or something that is brought on by financial necessity. . . . This is not something we do because we want to be different, or because we're rebellious to convention, but because our souls find a need for it.

(woman, thirty, married, big city, Canada)

Overall the journey into this way of life seems to be a relatively slow, evolutionary process, one that unfolds gradually over a period of months and years. The initial stages are a time of exploring and moving back and forth between traditional and innovative patterns of living and consuming. Gradually a person or family may find they have made a number of small changes and acquired a number of slightly different patterns of perception and behavior, the sum total of which adds up to a significant departure from the industrial-era way of life. One conclusion that I draw from these letters is that if change is too abrupt, it may not have the staying power to last. It seems better to move slowly and maintain a depth of commitment that can be sustained over the long haul.

The letters also revealed that the transition into this way of life is a personally challenging process. It may be accompanied by inner turmoil and feelings of uncertainty, self-doubt, anxiety, despair, and more. Life changes of this dimension seldom are made without deep soul-searching. The support of friends, family, and work associates is of great importance for transforming a stressful and difficult process into a constructive and shared adventure.

The path toward simpler living is further revealed in people's descriptions of how they consciously altered their everyday lives:

> . . . quit smoking, stopped eating meat, now run about eight miles a week, stopped shaving legs, stopped using scented products, stopped buying stylish haircuts, buy less clothing, buy looser, freer clothing, regularly take vitamins, gave away a lot of things, eat 90 percent more fruits and vegetables, meditate, walk a lot, read humanistic psy-

chology, study Sufism, feel strong affinity for all animals, weave, write.

(woman, thirty-three, single, big city, West)

I quit my forty-hour-a-week slavery and got a twenty-hour-a-week job that I love (working in a library). I started learning how to grow food in the city and make compost. I became conscious of what I was eating and how I was spending my money. I started learning to sew, mend, and shop secondhand, and I've stopped eating meat.

(woman, twenty-three, married, small city, West)

I do not own anything more than I need. The things that I do own are selected on the basis of their utility, rather than their style or the fact that they are currently faddish. I attempt to make things last. . . . I am nursing my car past 100,000 miles. I am doing political work, notably in opposition to nuclear power. . . . I am planning to build my own house, and the plans include small-scale technology aimed at promoting self-sufficiency, such as passive solar design, a greenhouse, composting toilets, windmills, and so on.

(man, thirty, single, suburb, West)

Changes include smaller house, wear clothes longer (except when in court; I'm a trial lawyer, feel it necessary to "play the role" when actually engaged in formal professional activity), recycle and buy secondhand when possible, bike and hike . . . live with a nice lady, have more time for children . . . human relationships, though fewer, are closer.

(man, forty-two, living together, rural, East)

I am doing what Bucky Fuller calls doing more with less. He also speaks of education as the process of "eliminating the irrelevant," dismissing all that is not furthering our chosen articulation of value—eliminating wasteful speech as well as costume, dietary habits as well as information addictions that do not further the evolution into that simple (not to say "noncomplex" but only "noncomplicated") life of adaptive progress to more and more diversified environments.

(man, twenty-seven, single, small city, East)

I recycle cans, bottles, and newspapers. We're very careful with water. . . . I buy used and handmade things as much as possible. . . . We've always been frugal in the way we furnish our house. We've never bought on time, which means we buy fewer things. We wear other people's hand-me-downs and we buy used furniture when possible. . . . A large percentage of our spending goes for classes (music, dance, postgraduate courses for my credential), therapy, and human-potential experiences.

(woman, forty-seven, married, big city, West)

We have a car but seldom use it, preferring to use bicycles because of a car's pollution and energy consumption. I am not into fashion and attempt to wear things till they are worn out—buy mostly serviceable work-type clothes, sometimes secondhand from friends. . . . Am vegetarian . . . belong to a food cooperative . . . everybody contributes four hours per month to working at the store/restaurant. This co-op forms an important hub in our community for most alternate social and spiritual activities. Learning about gardening . . . buy tools and appliances that are durable . . . avoid buying plastic and aluminum whenever possible. No throwaways . . . I attempt to use my buying power politically . . . strongly support appropriate technology . . . strongly motivated to understand myself and others—involved in meditation for awareness . . . the spiritual-search component is the major driving force in my life. . . . I always try to acquire new self-help skills: sewing, car repair, and so forth.

(woman, twenty-five, living together, city, Canada)

Greater simplicity frees time, energy, and attention for personal growth, family relationships, participation in compassionate causes, and other meaningful and satisfying activities.

INNER GROWTH AND VOLUNTARY SIMPLICITY

The term *inner growth* refers generally to a process of learning a natural quietness of mind and openness of heart that allows our interior experiencing to become apparent to us. It is a process of going behind our day-to-day labels and ideas about who we think we are in order to make friends with ourselves and the world. Here are some illustrative comments regarding the importance of voluntary simplicity to inner growth:

> I don't believe a person can make the commitment necessary to maintain this lifestyle without a spiritual-psychological motivation.
>
> *(man, thirty-three, single, small town, South)*

> It seems to me that inner growth is the whole moving force behind voluntary simplicity.
>
> *(woman, thirty-eight, single, suburb, West)*

> My life is suffused with joy, and that transforms even the ordinary day-to-day unpleasantries that come along. I've had a lot of years of growth pains and for a long time I got lost in the pain and suffered; but I've learned to let go more easily now, and even the hard stuff that comes along doesn't overpower the joy.
>
> *(woman, thirty-five, married, rural, West)*

> My husband and I . . . feel that our inner growth at this time is a daily way of life—tailored to our own particular situations. We know from life that one does not step in the same stream twice . . . thus, one keeps observing and relating to situations as they flow.
>
> *(woman, fifty-five, married, small town, West)*

I consider the whole picture one of positive personal growth that I inadvertently (luckily?) set in motion through trial and error and suffering. And now I sense a momentum established that I could not now "will" to halt.

(woman, thirty-three, single, big city, West)

I consider every moment a chance for growth. To pay attention and learn is my meditation.

(man, twenty-seven, married, rural, East)

In the opinion survey, people were asked if they were "now practicing or actively involved with a particular inner-growth process." The results, presented below, are striking. (Keep in mind that the percentages can exceed 100, since a person was asked to check those that apply and it was not uncommon for a person to be engaged in more than one growth process.)

- Meditation (e.g., Zen, Transcendental Meditation) 55%
- Other (e.g., biofeedback, "Intensive Journal") 46%
- Human potential (e.g., Gestalt, encounter) 26%
- Traditional religion (e.g., Catholicism, Judaism) 20%
- None 12%
- Psychoanalysis (e.g., Freudian, Jungian) .. 10%

A number of key findings emerge from this question. First, an overwhelming majority (88 percent) of the respondents indicated they were presently involved with one or more inner-growth process. Second, more than half of the respondents (55 percent) indicated involvement with some form of meditative discipline. In fact meditation appears to be the most prominent inner-growth process correlated with a life of conscious simplicity. Third, a near majority (46 percent) were involved with other, often highly personalized, inner-growth processes. The category "Other," as described in the letters, runs the gamut from keeping an intensive journal to the use of biofeedback, yoga, jogging, and many more. Fourth, although traditional religion is not unimportant with 20 percent actively involved, still it is not the primary focus for a group that is so strongly psychologically and spiritually oriented.

Inner growth is even more important to a path of voluntary simplicity than the foregoing statistics suggest. A number of persons who declined to identify themselves as being involved in any particular growth process explained why with comments such as these:

> I don't know what label to put on my inner-growth process. . . . I get high on a beautiful sunrise, a night when I sit alone on a chunk of granite and gaze up at billions of stars. . . . So what would you call it? I like to sit alone on a rock and just open my mind up to everything—would

you call it meditation? And I do believe in God and Christ, but for sure am not into traditional religion.

(man, twenty-four, single, rural, Midwest)

I am not actively involved in any particular growth process, but I'm always aware of the Spirit and how I'm part of it—gleaning what I can from traditional religions, yoga, and the insights provided to a clearer head since I've begun living more simply.

(man, twenty-two, single, rural, South)

I'm 75 percent spiritually oriented, though I haven't found a particular "path" outside of living simply and with love and searching.

(woman, eighteen, single, suburb, East)

I practice meditation and have a strong spiritual emphasis in my life that draws mainly from Christianity and Buddhism but also all other religions, and I do not practice any of them in any strict sense. I would call myself very strongly religious, but independent.

(woman, twenty-five, married, big city, Midwest)

. . . tried Zen, but it was wrong pace—but work constantly on self in a small, personalized manner.

(man, twenty-four, single, rural, West)

I do not deny taking ideas from many sources, but the result is fairly eclectic. The fact that most people I know do not fit me into a category seems to support this. So, my process would be individualistically developed inner growth: that which suits me personally.

(woman, twenty-six, single, big city, West)

The letters indicate a basic dilemma: When one's entire life is the inner-growth process, how can any one piece be singled out? The category "None" thus includes an undetermined, but substantial, number of persons for whom the inner-growth process is really "All."

Some said that they felt the category "Inner growth" was too limiting and that activities from political action and artistic creation to running should be considered legitimate vehicles for inner growth:

I am a radical and a feminist and believe that leading a simpler lifestyle and continuing political struggle is a form of personal growth left out of your analysis.

(man, twenty-nine, single, rural, West)

The inner growth you write of may be artistic, scientific, or social action, not just "spiritual."

(man, twenty-eight, single, small city, West)

Athletics is played down unjustifiably. For me, human potential has a physical as well as a spiritual meaning. Distance running produces a lot of the same vibrations that meditation evokes.

(man, twenty-nine, married, small city, West)

In short, just as there is no single "right" way to outwardly live more simply, so, too, there is no single "right" way to engage in the process of interior growth. Voluntary simplicity is a way of life that is compatible with Christianity, Buddhism, Hinduism, Taoism, Sufism, Zen, and many more traditions. The reason for this compatibility with diverse spiritual traditions is that simplicity fosters a more conscious and direct encounter with the world. And it is from the intimate encounter with life that there naturally arise the perennial experiences at the heart of all the world's great spiritual traditions.

THE IMPORTANCE OF RELATIONSHIPS

The involvement with inner growth may suggest an inward turning away from worldly relationships. To the contrary, it is the very deepening of insight through the inner quest that reveals the entire world as an intimately interconnected system. In an ecological reality—where everything is related to, and connected with, everything else—the quality and integrity of interpersonal relationships are of great concern. Or, as Martin Buber said, "All real living is meeting." This, too, is reflected in the letters:

We value our relationships more highly than anything else.
(man, twenty-nine, married, small city, West)

I feel good about everyday things, place more value and get *much* satisfaction from interpersonal relationships.
(woman, nineteen, single, suburb, West)

I feel this way of life has made my marriage stronger, as it puts more accent on personal relationship and "inner growth."
(man, twenty-seven, married, rural, East)

We are intensely family oriented—we measure happiness by the degree of growth, not by the amount of dollars earned.
(man, thirty-one, married, small town, East)

Satisfactions—growth through relationships with others and continuing personal contacts—the circle expands as more interests develop.
(man, twenty-nine, living together, small town, East)

This is not to portray a utopian situation. These are very human people. Many have confronted the fact that movement toward a fundamentally different way of life—involving change in both inner and outer worlds—can be challenging for relationships, even when there is a joint commitment to change. The varied nature of the stresses that may accompany movement toward voluntary simplicity is revealed in the letters:

We see some friends just grow old and tired of fighting [to maintain this way of life], especially when not backed up by solid love connections.

(man, thirty-four, married, rural, Canada)

I expect to [live more simply] in the future as I become more ingenious about dealing with differences in lifestyle preferences of my husband and myself and more firm about saying no to outside demands.

(woman, fifty-seven, married, suburb, West)

It is sometimes difficult or frustrating to fully live a life of simplicity because my partner is not as fanatically committed as I am to personal-growth exploration, nonconsumerism, and conservation. Satisfactions, however, are innumerable—I feel better physically, spiritually, and mentally.

(woman, twenty-eight, married, suburb, West)

I feel that I am alone with no support. Oh, some of my friends think that the things we are doing are admirable in a patronizing sort of way. Most people just think we're a little "nuts." I need some support. My wife is a somewhat reluctant supporter.

(man, thirty-six, married, big city, West)

My father and mother are supportive of our lifestyle; his parents are critical and don't understand—they are very money oriented. The kids sometimes worry that we are poor and compare themselves with their more conventional classmates.

(woman, twenty-nine, married, rural, West)

My choice of lifestyle, I feel, cannot infringe so much on my almost grown children's desires that it makes them miserable and rebellious. If they had all been toddlers when we began living this way, it would have been easier.

(woman, thirty-six, single, rural, East)

Clearly, movement toward simpler living has its tensions and stresses. For couples, the most frequently mentioned source of tension within a relationship arose when one partner was content with traditional patterns of living, consuming, relating, and working while the other partner wanted to explore nontraditional alternatives to one or more of them. For couples with children, the most frequently mentioned source of stress arose when the children felt themselves in a double bind between their traditional way of life that is shared by their peer group and an emergent way of life being explored by their parents.

Despite these stresses, relationships were described overall as an important source of nurturance, love, encouragement, reality testing, and support. Often this support extended beyond one's immediate family or friends to include a larger community of persons with whom there was a sense of kinship and spiritual bonding.

SIMPLICITY AND COMMUNITY

Many persons in this poll reported they felt tolerated by the larger community and actively supported by a smaller group of friends and associates. This is not surprising when we consider that many began adopting this way of life in the late 1960s and early 1970s—a time when the mood of most Western nations was not strongly supportive of a trend toward simpler living. Here is a sampling of the spectrum of experience reported in the letters:

> As for community support—I get both jeered at and cheered at—and some people even join in.
> *(woman, fifty-five, married, small town, West)*

> My motivations are understood by very few; I accept the responsibility for my actions.
> *(man, twenty-seven, married, rural, East)*

> I am greatly enriched by my lifestyle but sometimes feel alienated from society because of it. I consider it takes strong determination to stick to [my] convictions; sometimes frustrating because there are so many American dreamers.
> *(woman, twenty-seven, single, small town, West)*

I thought that the rural community would be a mecca of higher consciousness and have generally a spiritual atmosphere. Wrong! I have a problem finding people I have enough in common with that I can communicate with, but when I do, it's really dynamite!

(man, thirty-three, single, small town, South)

It is scary to live with less because for so long our society has said that money, possessions, and a career lead to security and happiness. I have a lot of support to make changes because of a tremendous community of people who are doing the same thing. The advantage is feeling more inner peace, increased self-acceptance, and community support.

(woman, twenty-nine, single, big city, Midwest)

Probably we will lead lives of greater simplicity to the degree that others in greater numbers in the society also start to do so. Community support is important.

(woman, thirty, married, big city, West)

The relative lack of community support was mentioned by many persons as being important in their degree of experimentation with alternative ways of life. Many of the pioneers of the simple life did not feel substantial support from the larger community or culture, but there is reason to think that mainstream values are shifting in a direction that is highly congruent with simplicity of living. If so, the sense of community support—so important in empowering individuals to move from sympathetic leanings to active involvement—could grow rapidly.

THE POLITICS OF COMPASSION

The political orientation of this group represents a break with mainstream politics. This is a strongly independent community of persons whose perspectives do not fit within the traditional spectrum of liberal and conservative politics. Among the U.S. respondents, only 1 percent labeled themselves Republicans. Some 28 percent said they were registered Democrats, but many included comments such as "out of lack of choice" or "would switch to something better." Overall there does not appear to be a strong sense of affiliation with either political party.

Roughly 60 percent of the sample placed themselves either in the category of "Independent" or "Other," and 11 percent declined to give any political orientation. The truly experimental character of the politics of this group is reflected in their responses to the category "Other." This brought write-in responses such as: *cooperativist, feminist, nonviolent activist, whatever works at the time, Libertarian, eclectic, decentralist, conservative anarchist,* and *apolitical but the weather may change.*

What seems to bind this group together is not political ideology but an appreciation for the dignity and preciousness of all life. Virtually nowhere in the letters was there any reference to traditional political ideologies; instead there was a sense that a whole new perspective is emerging that bridges between left and right, East and West, inner and outer, rich and poor, masculine and feminine.

> Our system causes us to be very political. . . . We are not a centralized movement. . . . Our concerns are for each other's survival. We communicate better than government and business. The "movement" is in reality a conscious choice of individuals—not a centralized program. . . . We are passing free ideas around, becoming independent through cooperation—young, old, brilliant, salt of the earth, revolutionary, conservative. We are the shakeout of the system, about to show the system how to improve itself. We communicate by learning and teaching. Call it the People's University, not a movement.
>
> *(man, thirty-five, married, suburban, East)*

> I am spending more and more of my time in various forms of community building and feel there are no political organizations, ideologies, or labels with which I am continually comfortable—except maybe voluntary simplicity.
>
> *(man, thirty-eight, single, small city, West)*

> Different aspects of [the simple life] have the potential of touching small parts of everyone's lifestyle, and it is this

feature that I feel gives hope to the movement. Voluntary simplicity has the potential of working on people like a chain reaction once the first spark is lit. On the other hand, I also see great potential for ecological disaster, social and political unrest, and ruin. I make no bets; I live from day to day and do what I can.

(woman, twenty-eight, married, suburb, West)

The fire ignited by combining lifestyle and politics is truly liberating and a joy to experience. Revolutions are made of such stuff.

(man, twenty-six, single, small town, West)

I don't think our lives will be very satisfying if we are divided and live in fear of others, regardless of what we may be able to accomplish with our inner lives. Thus if we are seeking genuine simplicity, we will have to operate in a way that will help others to gain awareness of their higher self-interest in what is happening to our planet and to ourselves as human beings.

(woman, fifty-five, married, small town, West)

For several reasons those choosing a simpler life seem more engaged politically than the general population. First, these individuals are taking control of their immediate life circumstances, and although this is limited, it is real and empowering. In small but cumulatively significant ways they are experiencing their own competence to make constructive changes, and this spills over into their lives as citizens.

Second, there is the realization that, even if they wanted to drop out, there is literally no place to escape the impact of a disintegrating global ecology. In an interdependent world there is not the option of being apolitical. Once we acknowledge the plight of the world, there is no place to go to retreat into our former ignorance.

Third, living with less is politically radicalizing. The survey revealed that those with higher incomes were more traditional in their political perspectives, whereas those with lower incomes were more innovative. When people choose to live closer to the level of material sufficiency, they are brought closer to the reality of material existence for a majority of persons on the planet. There is not the day-to-day insulation from material poverty that accompanies affluent living.

In various ways, many respondents said they did not want to drop out of politics, but rather to change their manner of participation. In general, people seemed more interested in local and global concerns than with national issues. Examples of local concerns were changing building codes to allow the use of innovative building designs and building materials. Examples of global concerns were actions to stop the destruction of rain forests and to preserve endangered species. Overall this is a political perspective that seems most concerned with building a sustainable future for all life on the planet.

Because the Greenpeace movement was mentioned as having the support of a number of respondents, its philosophy provides an insight into the politics of the simple life in the modern world:

> Ecology teaches us that humankind is not the center of life on the planet. Ecology has taught us that the whole earth is part of our "body" and that we must learn to respect it as we respect ourselves. As we feel for ourselves, we must feel for all forms of life—the whales, the seals, the forests, and the seas.[1]

The Greenpeace philosophy also provides a useful description of how the political concerns of those embracing ecological ways of life may become manifest as greater levels of nonviolent activism:

> The Greenpeace ethic is not only to personally bear witness to atrocities against life; it is to take direct action to prevent them. While action must be direct, it must also be nonviolent. We must obstruct a wrong without offering personal violence to its perpetrators. Our greatest strength must be life itself, and the commitment to direct our own lives to protect others.[2]

Many letters emphasized the importance of nonviolent means of resolving conflicts. However, pacificism should not be equated with passivity—a number of persons indicated they had participated in various nonviolent protest movements of the 1960s and 1970s.

Overall, where the traditional political perspective of Western industrial nations has tended to emphasize national interests, material concerns, and the legitimacy of violence in the conduct of foreign affairs, the politics of simplicity tends to emphasize planetary interests, a balanced regard for both material and spiritual development, and the importance of nonviolent means of resolving disputes. Other common themes in the letters were an emphasis on cooperation and sharing, self-reliance and neighborliness, human rights and social justice.

Contributions of the Feminine Perspective

The women's movement has made important contributions to both the growth and the character of simple living in the modern era. However, an affinity for a feminist perspective is no guarantee of sympathy for a simpler life. Many women have broken free of traditional sexual stereotypes but continue to embrace other stereotypes of Western industrial societies—particularly those concerning material success and social status. Nonetheless a substantial majority of those choosing a life of deliberate simplicity expressed a strong affinity for the spirit of the feminist movement. Here are some illustrative comments from the letters:

> I am becoming tuned to these ideas and lifestyle changes, partly as a feminist who sees a need for more bridges from the new age to feminism. . . . Behind this, of course, the relationship of our alienation/destruction of our mother, the earth, is parallel to our alienation/control of our mothers, the women.
>
> *(woman, thirty, married, big city, Canada)*

> I am a feminist—the women's movement gave me the strength and knowledge and confidence in myself and abilities to attempt this lifetime and lifestyle adventure. . . . I am especially supportive of women who want to "try their wings" and serve as an example of what a woman can do when she rejects prescribed roles and does "her own thing."
>
> *(woman, thirty-nine, living together, rural, East)*

> I took up voluntary simplicity after leaving my last (hopefully) male-dominated relationship, where I was supported financially by a man. A year of feminism and consciousness raising . . . convinced me that I would never be free to even know a man truly unless I could be free of dependency. . . . So supporting myself, seeing how I really wanted to spend my waking hours, coupled with the con-

cept of right livelihood, ecological awareness, yoga study, all led in one direction.

(woman, thirty-four, single, rural, West)

Another part of [simpler living] is more equally shared roles of men and women. Even though we have a child (which is often the determining factor in the traditional mother-stay-home, father-go-to-work family) we are attempting to not put ourselves in those roles. . . . Between us we share child care, meal fixing, cleaning, shopping, and money earning, while making sure our other needs are met (crafts, classes). For people without children this is even more the case.

(woman, twenty-two, living together, small town, West)

It is a way of life that made sense to me—nonmaterialistic, focused on people, cooperative, nonsexist.

(woman, twenty-seven, married, big city, Midwest)

Major changes include elimination of the "man is the chief breadwinner and boss" hang-up.

(man, thirty-eight, married, suburb, West)

The feminist movement has contributed to the growth of simpler living in several ways. First, feminism, by its example, has encouraged people of both sexes to explore alternative ways of living and working. When persons or groups empower themselves to act in ways that move beyond traditional roles and expectations, it provides an example of cultural liberation that all can emulate and translate into their unique circumstances. The liberation of women from sexual stereotypes has relevance far beyond women and sexual roles—it is a significant example of cultural liberation that applies to many other limiting stereotypes of traditional Western industrial societies.

Second, in liberating men from the need to perpetuate their half of the polarity of sex-based roles, feminism offers both men and women the freedom to be more authentically themselves. This has important implications for the male-dominated orientation of Western industrial societies, where the proof of "manhood" has often been equated with the ability to succeed in the material world. For many men consumption has served purposes far beyond that of meeting genuine material needs. High earnings and high consumption have been used as evidence of masculine competence, potency, and social status. With changes in male-female roles, other criteria of "success" can begin to emerge—criteria that are more balanced across both masculine and feminine qualities.

With greater balance between masculine and feminine qualities, our cultures would tend to become less aggressive, contain less disguised competition, be more receptive and open, have more supportive friendships, have a greater mixing of roles among men and women in accordance with innate interests and capacities, be able to nurture and care for others to a greater degree, place greater value on feeling and emotion, express greater concern for unborn generations, and have a stronger sense of the intimate interrelatedness of life. This integration and balance is crucial. If the masculine orientation—with its competitive, aggressive, dissecting, and materialistic approach to living—continues to dominate our perceptions and actions as a culture, we will scarcely be able to live in relative peace with the rest of the life on this planet. If we are to become whole persons in a cohesive culture, we must consciously integrate more feminine qualities into our lives. For many, a path of conscious simplicity involves the integration and balance of both masculine and feminine qualities into a coherent approach to living.

Voluntary Simplicity and Contributory Livelihood

Those who answered the survey had a variety of work backgrounds. Although for some, work seemed to provide little more than a source of income, for most it was a vehicle for participating in the world and a major source of satisfaction in living. Here are some illustrative comments from the letters:

To me the central reality of voluntary simplicity is the unity and interrelatedness of all aspects of my life. While my work has often been scheduled and distinct from the rest of my life, the more I get into the simpler life, the more I take my work home with me and involve all aspects and experiences of my life in my work. Work is something I do to make a living, but if it's not the kind of work that is also filling my need to feel that I'm contributing in a positive way to the welfare of at least some small part of humanity, I will find some way to make it contributory or find other work. It's like the Eastern perspective that a healthy life is all a meditation. The more you get into that kind of perspective, the more natural voluntary simplicity is, the easier it is to instinctively do what is going to be good for others and make you happy, and the more consistent and fulfilling your life is going to become.

(man, thirty-eight, single, small city, West)

It's important for people to realize that this lifestyle places no real boundaries between "work" and "play." "Work" is enjoyed and becomes simply a different activity than "play."

(woman, nineteen, single, suburb, West)

I live in grateful simplicity. The search for money (for its own sake) interferes in "loving work." For a time it seemed the solution was partial, a compromise between aesthetics and economics—between self-expression and survival. Now it seems that as artificialities are dropped, aesthetics becomes simple and natural—as life energy is released from survival and defense mechanisms, it enters a flow of abundance.

(man, twenty-nine, single, suburb, Midwest)

In work it takes another kind of energy and self-caring for "sanity" (rather than externally determined "success") to move away from the path that would take me "to the top." I know pretty clearly what the "top" is as defined by my colleagues. What I'm searching for is the "top" as defined by me.

(woman, twenty-eight, living together, small city, Midwest)

I recognized that the larger American culture did not sustain me with its consumerism and small jobs in large corporations.

(woman, thirty, living together, rural, West)

Commercialism is making people live on only the periphery of their whole beings. Things don't make you whole and happy, they can divide and disorientate. Putting all of oneself in a task makes you real—whole!

(woman, sixty-five, single, big city, Midwest)

The attitude toward work that is reflected in these comments seems to be that if we give less than our wholehearted participation to our work, then our sense of connectedness to life itself will be commensurately diminished. Work that is not strongly contributory may yield the income to feed our endless search for gratification, but such work seldom provides us with a sense of genuine contribution and satisfaction. Work that is largely self-serving will produce a feeling of alienation and unsatisfactoriness. However, when our work is life-serving, then our energy and creativity can flow cleanly and directly through us and into the world without impediment or interruption.

Overall, people viewed work as having at least four functions: first, as a means of supporting oneself in activity that is meaningful and materially sustaining; second, as an opportunity to support others by producing goods and services that promote a workable and meaningful world; third, as a context for learning about the nature of life—using work as a medium of personal growth; and fourth, as a direct expression of one's character and talents—as a celebration of one's existence in the world.

Given the drive to find meaningful work coupled with the shortage of such work in today's economy, it is not surprising that many choosing a simpler way of life are involved in starting their own small businesses. Among the various businesses mentioned in the letters were: restaurants, bakeries, bookstores, used-clothing stores, auto-repair shops, bicycle-repair shops, child-care centers, alternative health-care centers, craft shops, grocery stores, alternative schools, and more. This skilled and highly motivated group has ample talent to develop successful and compassionate businesses in communities across the country.

SATISFACTIONS AND DISSATISFACTIONS

Given the demands and stresses of this way of life, it would not be voluntarily chosen unless it was a satisfying way to live. Here is an illustrative sampling of responses to a question asking people to describe their satisfactions and dissatisfactions with living more simply:

> Dissatisfactions . . . are minute, not because they don't exist, but because they are part of the process—not obstacles but bumps on a road that I choose to follow.
> *(man, twenty-seven, single, big city, Midwest)*

> Satisfactions are the fulfillment of the heart. Dissatisfactions are the rumblings of the mind.
> *(man, twenty-eight, single, rural, West)*

> The most satisfying thing is that you can see life right in front of your nose—feel it all around you—running through you and continuing on. It's such a natural occur-

rence. . . . You gain access to parts of life that are otherwise inaccessible.

(woman, twenty-three, married, rural, East)

Satisfactions: I am my life. Dissatisfactions: There is always dissatisfaction; it precedes change.

(man, twenty-seven, married, rural, West)

Satisfaction is internal (not wanting and not rejecting), and I feel it when I am in touch with Reality or God. . . . I always get what I need. This renders my dissatisfactions irrelevant and meaningless (although I forget this often). So I can't bring myself to list my dissatisfactions because they're only a form of unfounded self-pity.

(man, thirty, married, rural, East)

There are no dissatisfactions, only difficulties, which can and will be overcome.

(woman, thirty-eight, married, suburb, East)

Satisfactions: Life is a lot simpler—I no longer spend twenty-four hours a month shaving legs and curling hair and God knows how long driving back and forth to Safeway. Life is infinitely cheaper—releasing money for the real luxuries of life. Dissatisfactions: outward appearances suggest poverty, and this culture is very discriminatory toward the poor.

(woman, twenty-eight, married, rural, West)

The greatest satisfaction derives from increasingly seeing the truth of one of the tenets of simplicity—my needs are always met, although my desires take a beating. . . . I begin to see that my satisfactions and dissatisfactions actually arise more from my attitude than circumstances. This for me is one of the most important aspects of voluntary simplicity . . . the state of consciousness associated with it.

(woman, thirty-two, single, city, West)

My life is less cluttered with "things" that control and befuddle me. Dissatisfactions? Only that it's sometimes the harder way to do something. . . . I can't rely on fast food, fast service, fast buying. Everything takes longer— cooking, buying, fixing. But it's worth it—most times.

(woman, twenty-seven, married, rural)

The satisfactions are of sharing and caring; of putting forth your best effort regardless of the results; of simply being happy . . . the rewards are immeasurably greater than those of possession or individual accomplishment. After a brief period of remorse for giving up the comfort and recognition that may have been attained, dissatisfaction with life seems to be experienced more infrequently and less intensely than before. As desires become fewer, frustration diminishes. As life becomes less ego-centered, it becomes more enjoyable.

(man, thirty-one, married, small town, West)

A most satisfying life in that we have a very close family relationship (our children are grown). We see that the children have developed values that are simple and allow for coping flexibly with the changing world. Using our own ideas and hands to make our way in both professions and home life is an exhilarating (and sometimes tiring) way to live.

(*woman, forty-seven, married, suburb, West*)

Satisfactions and dissatisfactions: The two sure go together! I can be so elated one day and down in the dumps when the progress is slow the next. Extrinsic joys are: (1) a marriage that works; (2) creating my own joys; (3) making my own music; (4) seeing my spiritual life blossom. Sorrows are just the bottom of the sine wave—when progress is slow.

(*man, twenty-five, married, small town, East*)

Satisfaction: Much more flexibility to move, grow, and generally bend with the winds. Continual improvement of my relationship with the universe. . . . In short, after thinking about it a minute my life has only improved since I began to consciously simplify everything. Aside from some complaints about others not understanding my lifestyle (my problem, not the lifestyle's) and a certain difficulty at making money (again, my problem) I have *no* complaints. . . . I feel more successful, wealthy, and healthy than I ever felt. And I mean wealthy in all senses.

(*man, thirty, single, small town, West*)

There are infinite satisfactions—primarily because I have consciously chosen to direct my life toward this lifestyle—

I am opening myself to growth, change, freedom of expression, caring for others. The major dissatisfaction—growth is painful!

(woman, twenty-eight, single, suburb, West)

The pervasive sense of satisfaction expressed in these letters is, I think, a direct result of people's learning to take control of their lives. Taking charge of one's life has many forms: learning basic skills that promote greater self-reliance (gardening, carpentry, repair skills, etc.), choosing work that is contributory and challenging, consuming in ways that respect the rest of life on this planet, and participating in compassionate causes. A growing capacity for self-determining actions contributes to the individual's sense of personal competence, dignity, and self-worth. A positive spiral of learning and growth unfolds from approaching life in this manner. As we become empowered to take charge of our lives, we feel that no one is to blame other than ourselves if our experience of life is not satisfying. And, in continually opening to and meeting that challenging responsibility, a new sense of freedom, aliveness, and satisfaction naturally emerges. Here is how E. F. Schumacher described people who, by conscious choice, were learning to live with less:

Many of them had a better time than they ever had in their lives because they were discovering the new freedom—the less you need, the freer you become. They discovered and kept discovering that they were carrying far too much baggage and so they dropped pieces right and left . . . and the more they dropped, the happier they became . . . and when they thought they had dropped nearly everything, they discovered that they were still needing and using and wasting more than the great majority of mankind.[3]

In contrast to this is the experience of many who have embraced a consumerist approach to life. When a person's primary objective is to maximize material pleasures while minimizing discomforts, then life becomes a constant process of "pushing" (trying to push away from discomforts) and "grabbing" (trying to acquire or hold on to that which gives pleasure). With the loss of inner balance that accompanies a habitual "pushing and grabbing" approach to life, a deeper pain ensues—that of becoming aware of the ultimate unsatisfactoriness of the pleasure-seeking/pain-avoiding process itself. With simplicity we can choose another path besides the continual back-and-forth struggle between pleasure seeking and pain avoiding. We can view life as a continual process of learning and challenge that will always include some measure of both pleasure and pain. By allowing both aspects to be present in our lives, we can choose a path that promotes our harmonious involvement in the web of life. The material pleasures of a balanced path may be fewer, but the overall satisfaction with life is, for many, far greater.

CONCLUSION

There are a number of conclusions that I draw from this survey of people choosing a life of conscious simplicity. First, a simpler way of life is not a utopian dream but a practical possibility. This is a down-to-earth and realistic approach to living that has already taken root in a number of developed nations. Given its emphasis on self-reliance and self-determination, it seems likely that this way of life has a tenacious foothold in these cultures.

Second, the pioneers of simpler living demonstrate by their example that we can each take control of our lives. We are not powerless in the face of ecological breakdown. We can take charge of our lives and create a far more workable and meaningful existence.

Third, an ecological approach to living involves much more than greater material frugality. Like spokes that reach out from the hub of a wheel, this way of life radiates outward from an inner core of experience to touch every facet of life.

Fourth, creative simplicity is in its springtime of development. Its current expression does not exemplify the culmination of this way of living; rather it represents its initial blossoming. A vast amount of work and learning yet remains before the potentials of this way of living will be fully apparent.

Fifth, there are no fixed norms that define this approach to living. The worldly expression of an ecological way of life is something that each person must discover in the context of his or her unique life circumstances.

Sixth, these pioneers of an alternative way of living reveal that "small is beautiful" when it comes to the process of making changes in our lives. Small changes that are seemingly inconsequential when viewed in isolation are of revolutionary significance in their cumulative impact. These many, small changes can accumulate, bit by bit, into a thorough transformation of our collective manner of living.

Seventh, many choosing a life of conscious simplicity are reasserting their capacity for citizenship and entrepreneurship. In turn, the traditional polarity of liberal and conservative (concerned primarily with the relative role and power of big government versus big business) is shifting toward another polarity—that of concern for the ability of the individual to determine his or her fate relative to the enormous power of *both* big government and big business. Traditional political and economic perspectives fail to recognize the most radical change of all in a free-market economy and democratic society: the empowerment of individuals to consciously take charge of their own lives and to begin making changes in their manner of work, patterns of consumption, forms of governance, modes of communication, and much more.

Eighth, this way of life does not represent a withdrawal from the world. Some may mistake the unwillingness of this forerunner group to participate in the aggressive exploitation of resources, the environment, and other members of the human family as a retreat from the world. Yet, far from withdrawal, a path of conscious simplicity promotes our intimate involvement with life. With conscious and direct involvement comes clarity. With clarity comes insight. With insight comes love. With love comes mutually helpful living. With mutually helpful living a flourishing world civilization is made possible. Rather than abandoning the world, those choosing a life of conscious simplicity are pioneering a new civilizing process.

THE PHILOSOPHY

OF SIMPLICITY

Chapter Three

✻

APPRECIATING LIFE

To live more voluntarily means to encounter
life more consciously. To live more simply is to encounter
life more directly. The "life" so encountered extends far
beyond that typically acknowledged in the daily social
routines of industrial societies. It is LIFE in its vastness,
subtlety, and preciousness that is the context within
which simpler living acquires its most compelling meaning and significance. To break through the superficiality
of a consumerist existence and deepen our appreciation
of life, we can remember that it is the universe that is
our home and that death is our ally.

THE UNIVERSE AS OUR HOME

Our universe extends through reaches of space that are so vast, and through aeons of time that are so long, that it outstrips the capacity of the human intellect to comprehend. The earth is part of a solar system that is millions of miles in diameter. Our solar system, in turn, is part of an enormous galaxy of some 100 billion stars arranged in a disk-shaped spiral some 100,000 light-years in diameter (that is as far as light can travel at the speed of 186,000 miles *per second* over the course of 100,000 years!). Despite its incomprehensible enormity our own galaxy is dwarfed by the larger known universe, which is estimated to contain more than 100 billion galaxies, each with hundreds of billions of stars.

Scientific research reveals that the universe is a wonderful and mysterious place. Indeed, modern physicists sound more and more like ancient mystics as they describe its nature. The seeming vacuum of "empty space" is now portrayed as being filled with immense amounts of energy; our vast cosmos is viewed as profoundly interconnected in ways that transcend all apparent separation in space and time; despite its monumental size, our cosmos is thought to have emerged from an area smaller than a pinpoint; matter is no longer viewed as being "solid" but, instead, is thought to be composed of whirlwinds of energy that flow together with such precision that they give the appearance of solidity; there is speculation that a black hole—an incredibly dense region where the normal laws of physics no longer apply—may lie at the center of many galaxies; and so on. We live within a masterfully designed cosmos of unimaginable subtlety, scope, and power. Einstein said, "The most beautiful and most profound emotion we can experience is the sensation of the mystical. It is the sower of all true science. He to whom this emotion is a stranger, who can no longer wonder and stand rapt in awe, is as good as dead."[1]

A miracle of creation surrounds us and intimately infuses every particle of our existence. American Indian lore speaks of our existence as a threefold miracle: the miracle that things exist at all, the miracle that living things exist, and the miracle that living things can become conscious of themselves.[2] Much of the time we take these three miracles for granted. We become desensitized and behave as if these three amazing facts of our existence were unimportant for the conduct of our everyday lives. Then, individually and culturally, we forget these miracles. Once forgotten by an entire culture, they are difficult to rediscover. Simplicity of living—encountering life more consciously and directly—facilitates that rediscovery.

Given the overwhelming vastness and miraculous nature of our universe, a natural tendency is to retreat into our socially constructed existence here on earth—a thin slice of reality that we can more readily comprehend because we are the primary architects of the cities and factories that now dominate our lives. Yet by ignoring the larger universe in which we are immersed—by concentrating our attention on the engaging and demanding social reality—we easily forget that it is the immense cosmos that is our true home. We live almost completely immersed in a socially constructed reality that so fully absorbs our energy and attention that virtually none remains to experience the wonder of our existence. The tragedy of modern industrial societies is the superficiality that they project (and that we accept) as the norm for human affairs. We unconsciously trivialize the human experiment with shallow pursuits of money and social status that mask the magnificence of what it means to be a human being.

It is important for us to remember where we live. As we encounter critical problems of global scale, we need a frame of reference for approaching the world as a whole system. We can acquire such a perspective by looking beyond the bounds of the earth to a larger universe. It is within the context of our experience as beings inhabiting a miraculous universe that the earth can be seen as a precious whole.

DEATH AS AN ALLY

Death is an important ally for appreciating life. I am not referring to a morbid preoccupation with death. Rather, I mean the felt awareness of our finitude as physical beings—an honest recognition of the short time we have to love and to learn on this earth. The knowledge that our bodies will inevitably die burns through our attachments to the dignified madness of our socially constructed existence. Death is a friend that helps us to release our clinging to social position and material possessions as a source of ultimate security and meaning. An awareness of death forces us to confront the purpose and meaning of our existence, here and now.

The way in which death can be an uncompromising friend to bring us back to the reality of life is revealed in the changing attitudes toward life of people who have had a "near death" experience. A common sentiment expressed by many near-death survivors is a decreased emphasis on money and material things and a heightened appreciation for nature and loving other people.[3] Dr. Kenneth Ring, a researcher of near-death experiences, quotes one woman survivor who said that after her experience, "I thoroughly enjoy life. Every day of it. As far as dying, if I were to die tomorrow that wouldn't bother me. But there is more of a thrill to life, each day of living . . . there is an inner feeling that life is terrific, great, fantastic—even on down days."[4]

Dr. Ring also quotes a young man who had a near-death experience after having been involved in a serious automobile accident. As a result the young man found that he developed an "awareness that something more was going on in life than just the physical part of it. . . . It was just a total awareness of not just the material and how much we can buy—in the way of cars and stuff, or food or anything. There's more than just consuming life. There's a point where you have to *give* to it and that's real important."[5]

Gandhi once said, "Just as one must learn the art of killing in the training for violence, so one must learn the art of dying in the training for non-violence."[6] If we are to lead nonviolent and loving lives, then we can begin by coming to terms with our own death. An appreciation that we must die awakens us from our social sleep and to the reality of our situation. Death is an unyielding partner in life—an inescapable certainty to push against as we sort out the significant from the trivial in our daily lives.

Consider the words of Nadine Stair of Louisville, Kentucky, who was eighty-five years old when she wrote the following entitled "If I Had My Life to Live Over":

> I'd like to make more mistakes next time. I'd relax. I would limber up. I would be sillier than I have been this trip. I would take fewer things seriously. I would take more chances. I would climb more mountains and swim more

rivers. I would eat more ice cream and less beans. I would perhaps have more actual troubles, but I'd have fewer imaginary ones.

You see, I'm one of those people who live sensibly and sanely hour after hour, day after day. Oh, I've had my moments, and if I had it to do over again, I'd have more of them. In fact, I'd try to have nothing else. Just moments, one after another, instead of living so many years ahead of each day. I've been one of those persons who never goes anywhere without a thermometer, a hot water bottle, a raincoat, and a parachute. If I had to do it again, I would travel lighter than I have.

If I had my life to live over, I would start barefoot earlier in the spring and stay that way later in the fall. I would go to more dances. I would ride more merry-go-rounds. I would pick more daisies.[7]

Finally, consider the wisdom from a now largely forgotten book, written in the United States in 1877. In its closing pages *The Royal Path of Life* describes a perspective on life that comes from an appreciation of death. Although written in a style of gracious eloquence that comes from an earlier era, it speaks plainly even today:

No sex is spared, no age exempt. The majestic and courtly roads which monarchs pass over, the way that the men of letters tread, the path the warrior traverses, the short and simple annals of the poor, all lead to the same place, all terminate, however varied their routes, in that one enormous house which is appointed for all living. . . . No matter what station of honor we hold, we are all subject to death. . . .

Ah, it is true that a few friends will go and bury us; affection will rear a stone and plant a few flowers over our grave; in a brief period the little hillock will be smoothed down, and the stone will fall, and neither friend nor stranger will be concerned to ask which one of the forgotten millions of the earth was buried there. Every vestige that we ever lived upon the earth will have vanished away. All the little memorials of our remembrance—the lock of hair encased in gold, or the portrait that hung in our dwelling—will cease to have the slightest interest to any living being.

We need but look into the cemetery and see the ten thousand upturned faces; ten thousand breathless bosoms. There was a time when fire flashed through those vacant orbs; when warm ambitions, hopes, joys, and the loving life pushed in those bosoms. Dreams of fame and power once haunted those empty skulls. . . .

A proper view of death may be useful to abate most of the irregular passions. Thus, for instance, we may see what avarice comes to in the coffin of the miser; this is the man who could never be satisfied with riches; but see now a few boards enclose him, and a few square inches contain him. . . .

Approach the tomb of the proud man; see the haughty

countenance dreadfully disfigured, and the tongue that spoke the most lofty things condemned to eternal silence. . . . Behold the consequences of intemperance in the tomb of the glutton; see his appetite now fully satiated, his senses destroyed and his bones scattered.[8]

These messages are clear. We cannot hide from death. Its embrace will consume our social existence entirely. Job titles, social position, material possessions, sexual roles and images—all must yield to death. This does not mean that we should abandon our material and social existence. Rather, it means that in consciously honoring the fact of our physical death, we are thereby empowered to penetrate through the social pretense, ostentation, and confusion that normally obscure our sense of what is truly significant. An awareness of death is an ally for infusing our lives with a sense of immediacy, perspective, and proportion. In acknowledging the reality of death, we can more fully appreciate our gift of life.

With the universe as our home and death as our ally, we turn to explore the two principal subjects of this section: the nature of living more voluntarily and the nature of living more simply.

Chapter Four

✵

LIVING MORE

VOLUNTARILY

To LIVE VOLUNTARILY REQUIRES NOT ONLY THAT WE BE
conscious of the choices before us (the outer world) but
also that we be conscious of ourselves as we select among
those choices (the inner world). We must be conscious
of both the choices and the chooser if we are to act
voluntarily. Put differently, to act voluntarily is to act
in a self-determining manner. But who is the "self" making the decisions? If that "self" is both socially and
psychologically conditioned into habitual patterns of
thought and action, then behavior can hardly be considered voluntary. Therefore, self-realization—the process of realizing who the "self" really is—is crucial to
self-determination and voluntary action.

The point is that the more precise and sustained is
our conscious knowing of ourselves, the more voluntary
or choiceful can be our participation in life. If we are

inattentive in noticing ourselves going through life, then the choicefulness with which we live will be commensurately diminished. The more conscious we are of our passage through life, the more skillfully we can act and the more harmonious can be the relationship between our inner experience and our outer expression.

Running on Automatic

To fully appreciate what it means to act voluntarily, we must acknowledge to ourselves the extent to which we tend to act involuntarily. We tend to "run on automatic"—act in habitual and preprogrammed ways—to a much greater extent than we commonly recognize.

Consider, for example, how we learned to walk as children. At first walking was an enormous struggle that required all our energy and attention. Within a few months the period of intense struggle passed. As the ability to walk became increasingly automated, we began to focus our attention on other things—reaching, touching, climbing. In the same manner we have learned and largely automated virtually every facet of our daily lives: walking, driving, reading, working, relating to others, and so on. This habitual patterning of behavior extends into the most intimate details of our lives: the knot we make in tying our shoes, the manner in which we brush our teeth, which leg we put first into a pair of pants, and so on. Not only do automatic patterns of behavior pervade nearly every aspect of our physical existence, they also condition how we think and feel. To be sure, there is a degree of variety in our thinking, feeling, and behaving; yet the variety tends to be predictable since it is derived largely from preprogrammed and habituated patterns of response to the world. If we do not become conscious of these automated patterns of thinking, feeling, and behaving, then we become, by default, human automatons.

We tend not to notice or appreciate the degree to which we run on automatic—largely because we live in an almost constant state of mental distraction. Our minds are constantly moving about at a lightning-fast pace, thinking about the future, replaying conversations from the past, engaging in inner role-playing, and so on. Without sustained attention it is difficult to appreciate the extent to which we live ensnared in an automated, reflexive, and dreamlike reality that is a subtle and continuously changing blend of fantasy, inner dialogue, memory, planning, and so on. The fact that we spend years acquiring vast amounts of *mental content* does not mean that we are thereby either substantially aware of or in control of our *mental process*. This fact is clearly described by Roger Walsh—a physician, psychiatrist, and brain researcher. His vivid description of the nature of thought processes (as revealed in the early stages of meditative practice) is so useful to our discussion that I quote his comments at length:

> I was forced to recognize that what I had formerly believed to be my rational mind preoccupied with cognition, planning, problem solving, etc., actually comprised a frantic torrent of forceful, demanding, loud, and often unrelated thoughts and fantasies which filled an unbelievable proportion of consciousness even during purposive behavior. The incredible proportion of consciousness which this fantasy world occupied, my powerlessness to remove it for more than a few seconds, and my former state of mindlessness or ignorance of its existence, staggered me. . . . Foremost among the implicit beliefs of orthodox Western psychology is the assumption that man spends most of his time reasoning and problem solving, and that only neurotics and other abnormals spend much time, outside of leisure, in fantasy. However, it is my impression that prolonged self-observation will show that at most times we are living almost in a dream world in which we skillfully and automatically yet unknowingly blend inputs from reality and fantasy in accordance with our needs and defenses. . . . The subtlety, complexity, infinite range and number, and entrapping power of the fantasies which the mind creates seem impossible to comprehend, to differentiate from reality while in them, and even more so to describe to one who has not experienced them.[1]

The crucial importance of penetrating behind our continuous stream of thought (as largely unconscious and lightning-fast flows of inner fantasy-dialogue) is stressed by every major consciousness tradition in the world: Buddhist, Taoist, Hindu, Sufi, Zen, and so on. Western cultures, however, have fostered the understanding that a state of continual mental distraction is in the natural order of things. Consequently, by virtue of a largely unconscious social agreement about the nature of our inner thought processes, we live individually and collectively almost totally embedded within our mentally constructed reality. We are so busy creating ever more appealing images or social facades for others to see, and so distracted from the simplicity of our spontaneously arising self, that we do not truly encounter either ourselves or one another. In the process we lose a large measure of our innate capacity for voluntary, deliberate, intentional action.

Bringing more conscious attention to our thought processes and behavior has profound social as well as personal implications. The late E. F. Schumacher expressed this forthrightly in his book, *A Guide for the Perplexed*: "It is a grave error to accuse a man who pursues self-knowledge of 'turning his back on society.' The opposite would be more nearly true: that a man who fails to pursue self-knowledge is and remains a danger to society, for he will tend to misunderstand everything that other people say or do, and remain bliss-

fully unaware of the significance of many of the things
he does himself."[2]

How are we to penetrate behind our automated and
habitual patterns of thinking and behaving?

LIVING MORE CONSCIOUSLY

The word *consciousness* literally means "that with
which we know." It has also been termed the knowing
faculty. To live more consciously means to be more consciously aware, moment by moment, that we are present
in all that we do. When we stand and talk, we know
that we are standing and talking. When we sit and eat,
we know that we are sitting and eating. When we do
the countless things that make up our daily lives, we
remember the being that is involved in those activities.
We remember ourselves (and to "re-member" is to make
whole; it is the opposite of dis-memberment). To live
consciously is to move through life with conscious self-
remembering.

We are not bound to habitual and preprogrammed
ways of perceiving and responding when we are consciously watchful of ourselves in the process of living.
Consider several examples. It is difficult to relate to another person solely as the embodiment of a social position or job title when, moment by moment, we are
consciously aware of the utter humanness that we both

possess—a humanness whose magnificence and mystery dwarfs the seeming importance of status and titles as a basis of relationship. It is difficult to deceive another person when, moment by moment, we are consciously aware of our unfolding experience of deception. It is difficult to sustain the experience of sexual desire by projecting a sexual fantasy when, moment by moment, we are conscious that we are creating and relating to a fantasy rather than the authentic individual we are with. In short, when we begin to consciously watch ourselves, in the activities of daily life, we begin to cut through confining self-images, social pretenses, and psychological barriers. We begin to live more voluntarily.

We all have the ability to consciously know ourselves as we move through life. The capacity to "witness" the unfolding of our lives is not an ability that is remote or hidden from us. To the contrary, this is an experience that is so close, so intimate, and so ordinary, that we easily overlook its presence and significance. An old adage states, It's a rare fish that knows it swims in water. Analogously the challenge of living voluntarily is not in gaining access to the conscious experiencing of ourselves but rather in consciously recognizing the witnessing experience and then learning the skills of sustaining our opening to that experience.

To clarify the nature of conscious watchfulness, I would like to ask you several questions. Have you been conscious of the fact that you have been sitting here reading this book? Have you been conscious of changes in your bodily sensations, frame of mind, and emotions? Were you totally absorbed in the book until I asked? Or had you unintentionally allowed your thoughts to wander to other concerns? Did you just experience a slight shock of self-recognition when I inquired? What does it feel like to notice yourself reading while you read; to observe yourself eating while you eat; to see yourself watching television while you watch television; to notice yourself driving while you drive; to experience yourself talking while you talk?

Despite the utter simplicity of being consciously watchful of our lives, this is a demanding activity. At first it is a struggle to just occasionally remember ourselves moving through the daily routine. A brief moment of self-remembering is followed by an extended period where we are lost in the flow of thought and the demands of the exterior world. Yet with practice we find that we can more easily remember ourselves—while walking down the street or while we are at home, at work, at play. We come to recognize, as direct experience, the nature of "knowing that we know." As our familiarity with this mode of perception increases, we get lost in thought and worldly activities less and less frequently. In turn, we experience our behavior in the world as more and more choiceful, or voluntary.

Bringing conscious attention into our daily lives may lack the mystery of searching for enlightenment with an

Indian sorcerer and the spiritual glamour of sitting for long months in an Eastern monastic setting, but consciously attending to our daily-life activities is an eminently useful, readily accessible, and powerful tool for enhancing our capacity for voluntary action.

EMBEDDED AND SELF-REFLECTIVE CONSCIOUSNESS

Because these two modes of consciousness are so crucial to our discussion, I want to define them more carefully. What follows is not an original distinction but an ancient one that has been variously labeled, but similarly described, by many others.[3]

The first mode of consciousness I will call embedded consciousness. Embedded consciousness is our so-called normal or waking consciousness and it is characterized by our being so embedded within the stream of inner-fantasy dialogue that little conscious attention can be given to the moment-to-moment experiencing of ourselves. In forgetting ourselves we tend to run on automatic and thereby forfeit our capacity for voluntary action. In the distracted state of embedded consciousness we tend to identify who we are with habitual patterns of behavior, thought, and feeling. We assume this social mask is the sum total of who we really are. Consequently we feel the need to protect and defend our social facade.

Having identified ourselves with this limited and shallow rendering of who we are, we find it difficult to pull away from our masks and freshly experience our identity.

The next step beyond embedded consciousness I will term self-reflective consciousness. Where the distinctive quality of embedded satisfaction is self-forgetting (running on automatic), the distinctive quality of self-reflective consciousness is self-remembering (acting in the world intentionally, deliberately, voluntarily). Self-reflective consciousness provides us with a mirror that reveals or reflects who we are as we move through our daily lives. This is not a mechanical watchfulness but a living awareness that changes moment by moment. It means that to varying degrees we are continuously and consciously "tasting" our experience of ourselves. Overall, the opening to self-reflective consciousness is marked by the progressive and balanced development of the ability to be simultaneously concentrated (with a precise and delicate attention to the details of life) and mindful (with a panoramic appreciation of the totality of life). Nothing is left out of our experience, as both the minute details and larger life circumstances are simultaneously embraced in our awareness.

To make friends with ourselves in this way requires that we be willing to accept the totality of ourselves—including our sensual desires, self-doubts, anger, laziness, restlessness, fears, and so on. We cannot move beyond the habitual pushes and pulls of these forces until we are conscious of their presence in our lives. In turn, to see ourselves in this manner calls for much patience, gentleness, and self-forgiveness, as we will notice ourselves thinking and acting in ways that we would like to think we are above or beyond. To the extent that we are able to see or know our automated patterns, we are then no longer bound by them. We are enabled to act and live voluntarily.

BEYOND SELF-REFLECTIVE CONSCIOUSNESS

The conscious evolution of consciousness does not end with becoming knowingly attentive to our everyday life experience. This is but a beginning of a much larger journey. Self-remembering is the immediately accessible doorway that gradually opens into the farther reaches of conscious knowing. By our being knowingly attentive to the "self" moving through our ordinary, day-to-day life experience, the entire spectrum of conscious evolution unfolds. Just as a giant tree grows from the smallest seedling, so, too, does the seed experience of self-reflective consciousness contain within it the farthest reaches of conscious evolution.

When we tune in to our moment-to-moment experiencing with persistence and patience, our experience of "self" is gradually though profoundly transformed. The boundaries between the "self-in-here" and the "world-out-there" begin to dissolve as we refine the precision with which we watch ourselves moving through life. The inner and outer person gradually merge into one continuous flow of experience. In other words, in the next stage beyond self-reflective consciousness the duality of "watcher and watched" merges into the unity of an integrated flow of conscious experiencing.

The capacity to ultimately experience the totality of existence as an unbounded and unbroken whole is not confined to any particular culture, race, or religion. This experience of ineffable unity is sometimes referred to as the Perennial Wisdom because it appears throughout recorded history in the writings of every major spiritual tradition in the world: Christianity, Buddhism, Hinduism, Taoism, Judaism, Islam, and more.[4] Each tradition records that if we gently though persistently look into our own experience, we will ultimately discover that who "we" are is not different or separate from that which we call God, Cosmic Consciousness, Unbounded Wholeness, the Tao, Nirvana, and countless other names for this ultimately unnameable experience. The common experience found at the core of every major spiritual tradition is suggested in the following statements:

The Kingdom of Heaven is within you.
    —words of Jesus

Look within, thou are the Buddha.
　　—words of Gautama Buddha

Atman (the essence of the individual) and Brahman (the ultimate reality) are one.
　　—words from the Hindu tradition

He who knows himself knows his Lord.
　　—words of Muhammad

The experience of unity or wholeness or love lies at the core of every major spiritual tradition. This does not mean there exists a universal theology; rather it means that we are all human beings and there are common experiences we share. For example, the capacity to experience love is not confined to any particular culture, race, or religion. It is a universal human experience. The theologian Paul Tillich described the ultimate nature of love as the experience of life in its actual unity.[5] If the experience of love is the experience of life in its actual unity, then consciousness is the vehicle whereby that experience is known. When we become fully conscious of life, we find that it is an unbroken whole and, in turn we may describe this experience of wholeness as "love."

Enabling Qualities of Living More
Consciously

There are a variety of ways in which the capacity for reflective consciousness is empowering and enabling. Being more consciously attentive to our moment-to-moment experience enhances our ability to see the world accurately. Given the distracting power of our thoughts (as lightning-fast movements of inner fantasy-dialogue), it is no small task to see things clearly. If we are not paying attention to our flow through life, then we will find that we have more accidents along the way, we will misunderstand others more often, and we will tend to overlook important things. Conversely, if we are being attentive to ourselves moving through the countless small happenings that comprise our daily lives, then we will tend to be more productive; we will tend to listen more carefully and understand more fully; we will have fewer accidents along the way; and we will be more present and available in our relationships with others.

Living more consciously has a straightforward and practical relevance, both for our lives as individuals and as a civilization in a period of stressful transition. As we develop the skills of living more consciously, we are able not only to examine the underpinnings of our personally constructed reality (as habitual patterns of thought and behavior), but additionally to examine our socially constructed reality (as equally habitual patterns of thought and behavior that characterize an entire culture). Socially, we are more able to penetrate through the political posturings, glib advertisements, and cultural myths that sustain the status quo. In an era dominated by hideously complex problems of global dimension, the ability to see the world more clearly is essential to the survival and well-being of the human family.

Developing the capacity for self-reflective consciousness also enables us to respond more quickly to subtle feedback that something is amiss. In being more attentive to our situation as a society, we do not have to be shocked or bludgeoned into remedial action by, for example, massive famines or catastrophic environmental accidents. Instead, more subtle signals suffice to indicate that corrective actions are warranted. In the context of an increasingly interdependent world—where the strength of the whole web of social, environmental, and economic relations is increasingly at the mercy of the weakest links—the capacity to respond quickly to subtle warnings that we are getting off a healthy track in our social evolution is indispensable to our long-run survival.

Further, living more consciously expands our range of choice and allows us to respond to situations with greater flexibility and creativity. In seeing our habitual patterns of thought and behavior more clearly, we have greater choice in how we respond. This does not mean that we will always make the "right" choices; rather,

with conscious attention our actions and their consequences become much more visible to us and they become a potent source of learning. And with learning
comes increasing skillfulness of action.

Reflective consciousness also promotes an ecological
orientation toward the rest of life. With conscious attention to our moment-to-moment experience, we begin
to directly sense the subtle though profound connectedness of all life. We begin to experience that the entirety
of existence is an unbroken whole. Awareness of our
intimate relationship with the rest of life naturally fosters
feelings of compassion. Our range of caring is expanded
enormously, and this brings with it a strong feeling of
worldly engagement and responsibility.

A witnessing or reflective consciousness has profound relevance for humanity's evolution toward a sustainable society. The ecological crisis we now face has
emerged, in no small part, from the gross disparity that
exists between our relatively underdeveloped inner faculties and the extremely powerful external technologies
now at our disposal. With humanity's powers magnified
enormously through our technologies, we can do irrep-
arable damage to the planet. The reach of our technological power exceeds the grasp of our inner learning.
Unless we expand our interior learning to match our
technological advances, we will be destined to act to the
detriment of ourselves and the rest of life on the planet.
We must correct the imbalance by developing a level of

interior maturation that is at least commensurate with the enormous technological development that has occurred over the last several centuries.

Just as the faculty of the human intellect had to be developed by entire cultures in order to support the emergence of the industrial revolution, so, too, must we now begin to develop the faculty of consciousness if we are to build a sustainable future. There are many paths for this journey of awakening. Whichever path is selected, we must begin to live more consciously as a species if we are to survive the coming decades and make a successful transition to some form of sustainable, global civilization.

THE NATURE OF HUMAN NATURE

Some people believe that "you can't change human nature," so the idea of an evolving human consciousness is no more than unwarranted idealism. Yet, what is human "nature"? The dictionary defines *nature* as the "inherent character or basic constitution of a person or thing—its essence." Does the inherent character and essence of a person ever change? We can gain insight into this key issue by asking an analogous question: Does the inherent character of a seed change when it grows into a tree? Not at all. The potential for becoming a tree was always resident within the seed. When a seed grows into a tree, it only represents a change in the degree to which its potential, always inherent in its original nature, is realized. Similarly, human nature does not change; yet, like the seed with the potential of becoming a tree, human nature is not a static "thing" but a spectrum of potentials. Human beings can grow from a primitive to an enlightened condition without that unfolding representing a change in our basic human nature.

There is, however, a crucial difference between the manner in which the tree and the person realize their innate potentials. For the seed to realize its full expression, it only has to find fertile soil, and the organic cycle of growth unfolds automatically. However, human beings do not develop in an equally automatic manner. For we humans to actualize our potentials, at some point there must be a shift from embedded to self-reflective consciousness (and beyond) if maturation is to continue.

Our culture provides the soil—either moist and fertile or dry and barren—within which we grow. However, the ultimate responsibility for growth, irrespective of cultural setting, remains with the individual. Overall, human nature is not a static condition but an unfolding spectrum of potentials. We can move along that spectrum without changing our basic human nature. That we do progress is vividly illustrated by the fact that humanity has moved from primitive nomad to the edge of global civilization in an instant of geological time. Despite the enormity and speed of our evolution of culture and consciousness, we are far from being fully developed. We are, I think, still in the adolescence of our species and have not yet begun collectively to imagine where our journey could lead in the future.

CONCLUSION

Throughout history few people have had the opportunity to develop their interior potentials consciously because much of the evolutionary journey of humanity has been preoccupied with the struggle for survival. The present era of relative abundance—particularly in industrial nations—constrasts sharply with the material adversity and poverty of the past. With simplicity, equity, and compassion we can have both freedom from want and the freedom to evolve our potentials in cooperation with other members of the human family. The Industrial Revolution may be viewed as a major breakthrough that could provide the material basis to support the pervasive evolution of individual and sociocultural awareness.

The cumulative effects of even a modest degree of development of the capacity for self-reflective consciousness would result, in my estimation, in a quantum increase in the effectiveness of self-regulating behavior that is conscious of, and responsive to, the needs of the larger world. The actions of countless individuals would arise from a deeper ground of shared awareness and this, in turn, would tend to produce a larger pattern of coherent and harmonious behavior. Self-reflective consciousness now moves from the status of a spiritual luxury for the few in a more rudimentary and fragmented social setting to that of a social necessity for the many in a highly complex and enormously enlarged social setting. Just as the faculty of the intellect had to be developed by entire cultures to support the emergence of the Industrial Revolution, so, too, I think, must we now begin to cultivate the development of the "knowing faculty," or consciousness, if we are to support the emergence of revitalized civilizations. No small part of our contemporary civilizational challenge is to acknowledge, and then begin consciously to develop, these vitally important potentials.

Chapter Five

☙

LIVING MORE

SIMPLY

IT MAKES AN ENORMOUS DIFFERENCE WHETHER GREATER simplicity is voluntarily chosen or involuntarily imposed. For example, consider two persons, both of whom ride a bicycle to work in order to save gasoline.[1] The first person voluntarily chooses to ride a bicycle and derives great satisfaction from the physical exercise, the contact with the outdoors, and the knowledge that he or she is conserving energy. The second person bikes to work because of the force of circumstances—this may be financial necessity or stringent gasoline rationing. Instead of delighting in the ride, the second individual is filled with resentment with each push of the pedals. This person yearns for the comfort and speed of an automobile and is indifferent to the social benefit derived from the energy savings.

In outward appearances both persons are engaged in identical activities. Yet the attitudes and experiences of each are quite different. These differences are crucial in determining whether or not bicycling would prove to be a workable and satisfying response to energy shortages. For the first person it would. For the second person this is clearly not a satisfying solution and perhaps not even a workable one (to the extent that he or she, along with many others, tries to circumvent the laws and secure his or her own personal advantage). This example illustrates how important it is whether our simplicity is consciously chosen or externally imposed. *Voluntary* simplicity, then, involves not only what we do (the outer world) but also the intention with which we do it (the inner world).

The nature of simplicity that I will focus on in this chapter is that of a consciously chosen simplicity. This is not to ignore a majority of the human family that lives in involuntary material simplicity—poverty. Rather it is to acknowledge that much of the solution to that poverty lies in the voluntary actions of those who live in relative abundance and thereby have the real opportunity consciously to simplify their lives and assist others.

THE NATURE OF SIMPLICITY

The dictionary defines *simplicity* as being "direct, clear; free of pretense or dishonesty; free of vanity, ostentation, and undue display; free of secondary complications and distractions." In living more simply we encounter life more directly—in a firsthand and immediate manner. We need little when we are directly in touch with life. It is when we remove ourselves from direct and wholehearted participation in life that emptiness and boredom creep in. It is then that we begin our search for something or someone that will alleviate our gnawing dissatisfaction. Yet the search is endless to the extent that we are continually led away from ourselves and our experience in the moment. If we fully appreciate the learning and love that life offers us in each moment, then we feel less desire for material luxuries that contribute little to our well-being and that deprive those in genuine need of scarce resources. When we live with simplicity, we give ourselves and others a gift of life.

We both seek and fear immediacy of contact with life. We search for aliveness, yet we mask our magnificence in a shell of material ostentation and display. We seek genuineness in our encounters with others and yet allow pretense and dishonesty to infuse our relationships. We look for authenticity in the world about us and find that we have covered our miraculous existence with layer upon layer of fashions, cosmetics, fads, trivial technological conveniences, throwaway products, bureaucratic red tape, and stylish junk. How are we to penetrate through these obscuring layers?

If you were to choose death as an ally (as a reminder of the preciousness of each moment), and if you were to choose the universe as your home (as a reminder of the awesome dimensions of our existence), then wouldn't a quality of aliveness, immediacy, and poignancy naturally infuse your moment-to-moment living? If you knew that you would die within several hours or days, wouldn't the simplest things acquire a luminous and penetrating significance? Wouldn't each moment become precious beyond all previous measure? Wouldn't each flower, each person, each crack in the sidewalk, each tree become a wonder? Wouldn't each experience become a fleeting and never-to-be-repeated miracle? Simplicity of living helps to bring this kind of clarity and appreciation into our lives.

An old Eastern saying states, Simplicity reveals the master. As we gradually master the art of living, a consciously chosen simplicity emerges as the expression of that mastery. Simplicity allows the true character of our lives to show through—like stripping, sanding, and waxing a fine piece of wood that had long been painted over. To further explore the broad relevance of simplicity, I will examine its worldly expression in three different areas: consumption, communications, and work.

SIMPLICITY AND CONSUMPTION

To bring the quality of simplicity into our levels and patterns of consumption, we must learn to live between the extremes of poverty and excess. Simplicity is a double-edged sword in this regard: living with either too little or too much will diminish our capacity to realize our potentials. Bringing simplicity into our lives requires that we discover the ways in which our consumption either supports or entangles our existence.

Balance occurs when there is sufficiency—when there is neither material excess nor deficit. To find this balance in our everyday lives requires that we understand the difference between our personal "needs" and our "wants." Needs are those things that are essential to our survival and our growth. Wants are those things that are extra—that gratify our psychological desires. For example, we *need* shelter in order to survive. We may *want* a huge house with many extra rooms that are seldom used. We *need* basic medical care. We may *want* cosmetic plastic surgery to disguise the fact that we are getting older. We *need* functional clothing. We may *want* frequent changes in clothing style to reflect the latest fashion. We *need* a nutritious and well-balanced diet. We may *want* to eat at expensive restaurants. We *need* transportation. We may *want* a new Mercedes.

Only when we are clear about what we need and what we want can we begin to pare away the excess and find a middle path between extremes. No one else can find this balance for us. This is a task that we each must do for ourselves.

The hallmark of a balanced simplicity is that our lives become clearer, more direct, less pretentious, and less complicated. We are then empowered by our material circumstances rather than enfeebled or distracted. Excess in either direction—too much or too little—is complicating. If we are totally absorbed in the struggle for subsistence or, conversely, if we are totally absorbed in the struggle to accumulate, then our capacity to participate wholeheartedly and enthusiastically in life is diminished.

Four consumption criteria, developed by a group in San Francisco while exploring a life of conscious simplicity, go to the very heart of the issue of balanced consumption:

- Does what I own or buy promote activity, self-reliance, and involvement, or does it induce passivity and dependence?

- Are my consumption patterns basically satisfying, or do I buy much that serves no real need?

- How tied are my present job and lifestyle to installment payments, maintenance and repair costs, and the expectations of others?

- Do I consider the impact of my consumption patterns on other people and on the earth?[2]

This compassionate approach to consumption stands in stark contrast to the industrial-era view, which assumes that if we increase our consumption, we will increase our happiness. However, when we equate our identity with that which we consume—when we engage in "identity consumption"—we become possessed by our possessions. We are consumed by that which we consume. Our identity becomes not a free-standing, authentic expression in the moment, but a material mask that we have constructed so as to present a more appealing image for others to see. The vastness of who we are is then compressed into an ill-fitting shell that obscures our uniqueness and natural beauty. When we believe the advertiser's fiction that "you are what you consume," we begin a misdirected search for a satisfying experience of identity. We look beyond ourselves for the next thing that will make us happy: a new car, a new wardrobe, a new job, a new hairstyle, a new house, and so on. Instead of lasting satisfaction, we find only temporary gratification. After the initial gratification subsides, we must begin again—looking for the next thing that, this time, we hope will bring some measure of enduring satisfaction. Yet the search is both endless and hopeless because it is continually directed away from the "self" that is doing the searching. If we were to pause in our search and begin to discover that our true identity is much larger than any that can be fashioned through even the most opulent levels of material consumption, then the entire driving force behind our attempts at "identity consumption" would be fundamentally transformed.

It is transformative to withdraw voluntarily from the preoccupations with the material rat race of accumulation and instead accept our natural experience—unadorned by superfluous goods—as sufficient unto itself. It is a radical simplicity to affirm that our happiness cannot be purchased, no matter how desperately the advertiser may want us to believe the fiction that we will never be happy or adequate without his or her product. It is a radical simplicity when we accept our bodies as they are—when we affirm that each of us is endowed with a dignity, beauty, and character whose natural expression is infinitely more interesting and engaging than any imagined identity we might construct with layers of stylish clothes and cosmetics.

A conscious simplicity, then, is not self-denying but life-affirming. Voluntary simplicity is not an "ascetic simplicity" (of strict austerity); rather it is an "aesthetic simplicity" where each person considers whether his or her level and pattern of consumption fits with grace and integrity into the practical art of daily living on this planet. The possessions that seemed so important and appealing during the industrial era would gradually lose much of their allure. The individual or family who, in the past, was admired for a large and luxurious home would find that the mainstream culture increasingly admired those who had learned how to combine functional simplicity and beauty in a smaller home. The person who was previously envied for his or her expensive car would find that a growing number of people were uninterested in displays of conspicuous consumption. The person who was previously recognized for always wearing the latest in clothing styles would find that more and more people viewed high fashion as tasteless ostentation that was no longer fitting in a world of great human need. This does not mean that people would turn away from the material side of life; rather, they would place a premium on living ever more lightly and aesthetically.

Some are concerned that ecological ways of living will undermine economic activity and produce high unemployment. This seems unfounded. Most of those choosing ecological ways of living are very intent upon leading purposeful lives that respond to the real needs of others. When we look around at the condition of the world, we see a huge number of unmet needs: urban renewal, environmental restoration, education of illiterate and unskilled youth, repair of decaying roads and bridges, provision of child care and health care, and many more. Because there are an enormous number of unmet needs, there are an equally large number of purposeful and satisfying jobs waiting to get done. The difficulty is that in many industrialized nations there is such an overwhelming emphasis placed on individual consumption that it has resulted in the neglect of work that promotes the public welfare. There will be no shortage of employment opportunities in an ecologically oriented economy. In moving toward simpler ways of living and a needs-oriented economy that does not artificially inflate consumer wants, an abundance of meaningful and satisfying jobs will become available along with the additional resources needed to pay for them.

The earth does not have sufficient resources and environmental carrying capacity to allow all of the people in the world to consume at the levels, and in the forms, that have characterized industrial growth in the West. We need much more efficient forms of development— marked by frugality and ecological integrity. Food production, housing, transportation, energy production, and many more areas of our lives will have to be diversely and creatively adapted if we are to sustain the process of global development in the twenty-first century. We must choose levels and patterns of consumption that are globally sustainable—that use the world's resources wisely and do not overstress the world's ecology. Simplicity of living has enormous relevance for meeting these challenges.

SIMPLICITY AND INTERPERSONAL COMMUNICATIONS

The ability to communicate is at the very heart of human life and civilization. If we cannot communicate effectively, then civilization itself is threatened. If we apply the principle of simplicity to our communications, then they will tend to be more direct, clear, and honest. In this respect consider five areas where simplicity can enhance the quality of communication.

First, to communicate more simply means to communicate more honestly—it is to connect our inner experience with our outer expressions. Integrity, authenticity, and honesty encourage the development of trust. With trust there is a basis for cooperation, even when there remain disagreements. With cooperation there is a foundation for mutually helpful living. Simplicity of communication, then, is vital for building a sustainable future.

Second, simplicity of communication implies that we will let go of wasteful speech and idle gossip. Wasteful speech can assume many forms: distracted chatter about people and places that have little relevance to what is happening in the moment; name-dropping to build social status; using unnecessarily complex language or overly coarse language; and so on. When we simplify our communications by eliminating the irrelevant, we infuse what we do communicate with greater importance, dignity, and intention.

Third, simplicity is also manifest in communication by valuing silence. The revered Indian sage Ramana Maharshi said that silence speaks with "unceasing eloquence."[3] When we appreciate the power and eloquence of silence, our exchanges with others come into sharper focus. The sometimes painful or awkward quality that silence brings in social settings is, I think, a measure of the mismatch between our social facades and our more authentic sense of self. Once we are comfortable in allowing silence its place in communication, there is the opportunity to express ourselves more fully and authentically. The simplicity of silence fosters dignity, depth, and directness in communication.

Fourth, simplicity is also expressed in communication as greater eye contact with others. Because the eyes have been called the seat of the soul, it is not surprising that more direct eye contact with others tends to cultivate more soulful communication. This does not mean engaging others with a tight, hard, and demanding gaze; rather, we can approach others with "soft eyes" that are gentle and accepting. When we directly "see" another in this way, there is often a mutual flash of recognition. The source of that shared awareness resides not in the pigmented portion of the eyes, but within the darkness of the interior center—therein is the place that yields the spark of conscious recognition. It is the dancing and brilliant darkness of the interior eye that reveals that the essence of "self" and "other" arise from the same source. Emerson spoke eloquently of how poverty, riches, status, power, and sex are all forms whose veil yields to our knowing eyes. What is seen goes beyond all of these forms and labels to reveal the very essence of who we are.

Fifth, simplicity can also be expressed in our communications as greater openness to nonsexual physical contact. Hugging and touching that is free from disguised sexual manipulation is a powerful way of more fully and directly communicating with another. Studies have shown that a strong correlation exists between acceptance of physical touching and a tendency toward gentleness.[4] If we are to learn to live together as a global family, then we must learn to touch one another with less physical and psychological violence.

SIMPLICITY AND WORK

A third major example of the relevance of simplicity is how it can transform our approach to work. Our relationship with our work is enhanced greatly when our livelihood makes a genuine contribution both to ourselves and to the human family. It is through our work that we develop our skills, relate with others in shared tasks, and contribute to the larger society.

Thomas Aquinas said, "There can be no joy of life without joy of work." Our joy of work and life can flourish when we move from an intention of "making a killing" for ourselves to that of "earning a living" in a way that contributes to the well-being of all. In sensing and responding to the needs of the world, our work acquires a natural focus and intention that brings clarity and satisfaction into our lives.

Simplicity is also manifest in more human-sized places of employment. Many persons work within massive bureaucracies: huge corporations, vast government agencies, enormous educational institutions, sprawling medical complexes, and so on. These workplaces have grown so large and so complex that they are virtually incomprehensible, both to those who work within them and to those who are served by them. Not surprisingly the occupations that often emerge from these massive organizations tend to be routinized, specialized, and stress producing. Simplicity in this setting implies a change in favor of more human-sized workplaces. This does not mean abandonment of the institutions that have arisen during the industrial era; instead, it means that we would redesign organizations in such a way that they are of more comprehensible size and manageable complexity. By consciously creating workplaces of a size that encourages meaningful involvement and personal responsibility, the rampant alienation, boredom, and emptiness of work would be greatly reduced.

The quality of simplicity can also be expressed as more direct and meaningful participation in decisions about work—for example, direct participation in decisions about what to produce; direct involvement in organizing the work process; and direct participation in deciding the structure of working arrangements (such as flexible hours, job sharing, job swapping, team assembly, and other innovations).

In looking at three very different areas—consumption, communications, and work—it is evident that simplicity has pervasive relevance that can touch and transform every facet of our lives.

VOLUNTARY SIMPLICITY: AN INTEGRATED PATH FOR LIVING

To live more voluntarily is to live more consciously. To live more consciously is to live in a "life-sensing" manner. It is to "taste" our experience of life directly as we move through the world. It is to open consciously—as fully, patiently, and lovingly as we are able—to the unceasing miracle of our "ordinary" existence.

To live more simply is to live in harmony with the vast ecology of all life. It is to live with balance—taking no more than we require and, at the same time, giving fully of ourselves. To live with simplicity is by its very nature a "life-serving" intention. Yet, in serving life, we serve ourselves as well. We are each an inseparable part of the life whose well-being we are serving. In participating in life in this manner, we do not disperse our energy frivolously but employ our unique capacities in ways that are helpful to the rest of life.

Voluntary simplicity, as a life-sensing and life-serving path, is neither remote nor unapproachable. This way of life is always available to the fortunate minority of the world who live in relative affluence. All that is required is our conscious choosing. This path is no farther from us than we are from ourselves. To discover our unique understanding and expression of this path does not require us to start from anywhere other than where we already are. This path is not the completion of a journey but its continual beginning anew. Our task is to open freshly to the reality of our situation as it already is and then to respond wholeheartedly to what we experience. The learning that unfolds along the path of our life-sensing and life-serving participation in the world is itself the journey. The path itself is the goal. Ends and means are inseparable.

A self-reinforcing spiral of growth begins to unfold for those who choose to participate in the world in a life-sensing and life-serving manner. As we live more consciously, we feel less identified with our material possessions and thereby are enabled to live more simply. As we live more simply and our lives become less filled with unnecessary distractions, we find it easier to bring our undivided attention into our passage through life, and thereby we are enabled to live more consciously.

Each aspect—living more voluntarily and living more simply—builds upon the other and promotes the progressive refinement of each. Voluntary simplicity fosters:

- A progressive refinement of the social and *material* aspects of life—learning to touch the earth ever more lightly with our material demands; learning to touch others ever more gently and responsively with our social institutions; and learning to live our daily lives with ever less complexity and clutter.

- A progressive refinement of the *spiritual* or consciousness aspects of life—learning the skills of touching the world ever more lightly by progressively releasing habitual patterns of thinking and behaving that make our passage through life weighty and cloudy rather than light and spacious; learning how to "touch and go"—to not hold on—but to allow each moment to arise with newness and freshness; and learning to be in the world with a quiet mind and open heart.

By simultaneously evolving the material and the spiritual aspects of life in balance with one another—allow-

ing each to inform the other synergistically—we pull
ourselves up by our own bootstraps. Gradually the experience of being infuses the process of doing. Life-
sensing and life-serving action become one integrated
flow of experience. We become whole. Nothing is left
out. Nothing is denied. All faculties, all experience, all
potentials are available in the moment. And the path
ceaselessly unfolds.

Simplicity and Social Renewal

Chapter Six

✄

CIVILIZATIONS IN

TRANSITION

JUST AS WE HUMANS EVOLVE THROUGH MAJOR STAGES of development, so, too, do civilizations. Like the inexorable passing of seasons, civilizations also pass through their seasons of growth and decline. In my judgment a number of industrial civilizations have already passed through their spring and summer of growth and have entered their autumn and winter of decline. Unless creative actions are taken soon to move beyond the industrial era, we will move deep into a harsh winter of civilizational breakdown.

The signs that mark our entry into a stage of civilizational crisis are many; for example, debt-burdened and stagnating economies, the loss of a compelling sense of social purpose, special-interest groups that override the public interest and create political gridlock, overwhelming bureaucratic complexity, the inability to respond to critical problems in the local to global ecology. These challenges are so severe that industrial-era civilizations must make fundamental changes if they are to survive. We require new ways of living and a new sense of social purpose that again draws out our wholehearted and enthusiastic participation in life. It is no accident that experiments in simpler living are blossoming at the very time that industrial-era ways of living have entered a time of crisis. Ecological ways of living will provide an essential foundation for building postindustrial civilizations.

Four Stages of Civilizational Growth

It is psychologically demanding to consider the breakdown and transformation of civilizations. This is not an abstract process, as we are the persons who must live through it. To venture into this realm of inquiry may bring—as it has for me—considerable psychological discomfort. All of the hopes and fears that lie in uneasy though quiet repose in our everyday lives become starkly visible as we consider the depth and scope of change that lies ahead. Our anxiety about transformative civilizational change is lessened when we realize that it is part of a natural and purposeful process. To see the organic nature of social evolution, we need to separate the deeper currents of change from the surface turbulence that occupies so much of our public attention. We can do this by looking at the seasons or stages of development to see more clearly where we are in the life cycle of civilizational growth and decline.

Shown below is a theory of civilizational growth I developed that describes four seasons of development.* This theory is in accord with the general principle articulated by world historian Arnold Toynbee, who said, "A growing civilization may be defined as one in which the components of its culture are in harmony with each other and form an integral whole; on the same principle, a disintegrating civilization can be defined as one in which these same elements have fallen into discord."[1] Here are the primary stages, and patterns of harmony and discord, that I see in the unfolding of industrial-era civilizations.

*This model of development is based upon research that I conducted to describe the behavioral properties of social systems as they grow in size and complexity. See the report *Limits to the Management of Large, Complex Systems,* which I prepared for the President's Science Advisor and the National Science Foundation; SRI International, Menlo Park, Calif., February 1977. Or see the summary article coauthored with Robert Bushnell, "Limits to the Management of Complexity: Are Bureaucracies Becoming Unmanageable?" in *The Futurist,* Washington, D.C., December 1977. The theory underlying this model is also described at length in Appendix III of the first edition of *Voluntary Simplicity* (New York: William Morrow, 1981), "An Overview of the Race with Complexity and Stages of Growth."

Table 2: Four Stages of Growth in the Life Cycle of Western Industrial Civilizations

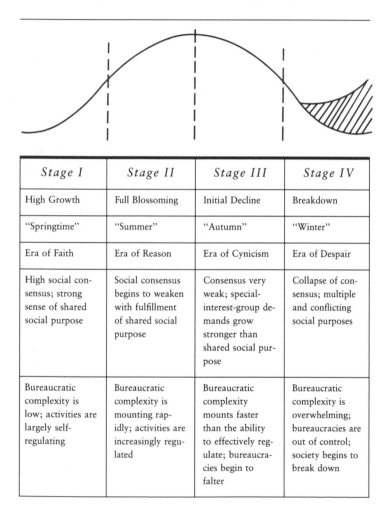

Stage I	Stage II	Stage III	Stage IV
High Growth	Full Blossoming	Initial Decline	Breakdown
"Springtime"	"Summer"	"Autumn"	"Winter"
Era of Faith	Era of Reason	Era of Cynicism	Era of Despair
High social consensus; strong sense of shared social purpose	Social consensus begins to weaken with fulfillment of shared social purpose	Consensus very weak; special-interest-group demands grow stronger than shared social purpose	Collapse of consensus; multiple and conflicting social purposes
Bureaucratic complexity is low; activities are largely self-regulating	Bureaucratic complexity is mounting rapidly; activities are increasingly regulated	Bureaucratic complexity mounts faster than the ability to effectively regulate; bureaucracies begin to falter	Bureaucratic complexity is overwhelming; bureaucracies are out of control; society begins to break down

Stage I: High Growth

This is the "springtime" of civilizational growth. It is an era of faith in basic values. The majority of people share a coherent and compelling image of future potentials for growth. This is a period of great vitality, creativity, innovation, and experimentation as people seek to realize those potentials. The established social order has great legitimacy and is sufficiently uncomplicated so as to be comprehensible to the majority. People have a relatively high degree of access to their leaders. Activities are self-regulating to a significant extent. There is an implicit faith in the appropriateness of seeking a higher material standard of living as a paramount personal and social goal.

Stage II: Full Blossoming

This is the "summertime" of growth for industrial civilizations. The material promise of the industrial view of the world reaches its fullest blossoming in this period. As the social order becomes increasingly complex and the need for rational management grows, this becomes an era of reason more than faith. The time of entrepreneurial creativity has passed, and we have moved into a period of managed creativity. Creativity is still present, but it is increasingly channeled into acceptable institutional forms. The bursts of vitality and innovation of Stage I have been replaced by a more methodical process of planning and implementation. With the rapid growth in the size and complexity of all institutions—in both government and business—people find themselves increasingly removed from access to leadership and often feel dwarfed by these massive organizations. Yet this seems a small price to pay for the extraordinary benefits and achievements that accompany this period of growth. Growth continues throughout the entire period but at a steadily decreasing rate. As we approach the end of this period, the industrial-era goals are increasingly fulfilled and social consensus weakens commensurately.

Stage III: Initial Decline

This is the "autumn" of growth for industrial civilizations. With the fulfillment of the promise of the industrial era, social consensus begins to dissolve. Special-interest-group demands grow stronger as the sense of shared social purpose grows weaker. Not surprisingly this is an era of cynicism and skepticism. Faith in the appropriateness of the historical civilizational agenda of ever-increasing material growth is eroded. The entire culture is losing both its drive and its sense of direction. The dream of material abundance and ease is rapidly becoming a nightmare of unexpected problems and overwhelming bureaucratic regulation. The powerful engine of economic and technological growth is running out of steam. The "social glue"—a compelling sense of social purpose—that has held the industrial culture together is rapidly dissolving. Institutions in every sector of society are faltering under the weight of mounting bureaucratic complexity. Leaders are so bogged down in coping with institutional crises that they have little time to reflect on the larger pattern of forces at work. The visionary capacity of the culture is being rapidly exhausted as leaders are unable to rise above the demands of crisis management and envision an alternative course of social activity that will again draw out the enthusiastic participation of the citizenry. Unexpected problems are cropping up everywhere. At the same times the pervasively bureaucratized society is losing its resilience and is becoming more vulnerable to disruption. Faith in the basic soundness of institutions is eroding, and trust in the leadership to solve problems is rapidly declining. Some people seek representation by special-interest groups in an attempt to ensure their own well-being, even though it may be at the expense of the larger social welfare. Leaders are more tolerated than actively supported. People feel divorced from their leadership and powerless to make fundamental changes. The costs of running the massive bureaucracies that dominate every sector of society are mounting rapidly. The performance of the whole social apparatus is declining.

Stage IV: Breakdown

This is the "winter" of growth for industrial civilizations. It is an era of despair as all hope that things can return to their former status is exhausted. All of the problems of Stage III are present, but the problems are now more intense. Social and bureaucratic complexity has reached overwhelming levels. The society and its institutions are no longer comprehensible and are increasingly out of control. Social consensus and a shared sense of social purpose have all but vanished. Political and social relations are in chaos. With the collapse of consensus, multiple and conflicting social purposes compete with one another for dominance. There is a rapid turnover of leaders, ideologies, and policy solutions; yet nothing seems to work for long. Every attempt to restore some semblance of order is quickly overwhelmed by mounting levels of disorder. Leaders govern virtually without support. The regulatory apparatus that held the faltering social system together in Stage III is now unable to cope with the overwhelming complexity, the loss of social legitimacy, the unexpected problems that abound, and the absence of compelling social purpose. The remaining creativity, vitality, ingenuity, and resiliency of the entire social apparatus are being rapidly exhausted in a grinding downward spiral into bureaucratic confusion and chaos. The situation has become intolerable and untenable. The need for fundamental change is inescapable.

WHERE ARE WE NOW?

If we accept these four stages of growth as a useful approximation of the cycle of industrial civilizations, the question naturally arises, Which stage of this life cycle are we in now? In my judgment, the United States and many other industrial nations are, as of the early 1990s, moving into the Stage IV region of systems breakdown.

There is considerable evidence to support the assertion that many industrialized nations have moved from the autumn into the winter of growth. Chapter 1 described a long list of problems facing developed nations and the world. In summary, if we continue along our present course, children alive today will inhabit a warming world whose climate is so destabilized that it disrupts food production and results in massive waves of starvation; a planet with easily accessible supplies of petroleum depleted; with widespread deforestation; with the goodwill of the human family ravaged as nations fight over access to remaining resources; with coastal cities inundated by rising seas; with millions of people migrating to resource-favored nations and regions; with solar radiation penetrating through a weakened ozone layer and threatening the earth's food chain; with far less farmland and productive topsoil to feed an additional 3 billion people; with a drastically reduced number of plant and animal species; and with toxic pollution spread throughout the land, water, and air. In short, unless dramatic changes are made in our manner of living and consuming, we will create a world filled with immense destruction, suffering, conflict, and despair.

These problems are of enormous *scale* (often involving millions or billions of people), *complexity* (of bewildering difficulty to comprehend), and *severity* (failure to cope with any one of them will result in monumental human suffering). We confront many different kinds of challenges: *technical* problems (coping with energy and resource shortages), *normative* problems (discovering values beyond materialism that draw people together with a sense of shared purpose), and *process* problems (finding ways for millions of citizens to interact with massively complex institutions from the local to the global scale). These individual problems comprise a tightly interdependent and *intertwined system of problems* that cannot be dealt with on a one-by-one basis; instead they require a dramatic shift in our overall pattern of thinking and living. In sum, many industrial nations have already passed through their autumn and have entered their winter of development—the stage of systems breakdown.

It is important not to equate the successful fulfillment of the potentials of the industrial era with failure. Instead, movement into the stage of civilizational breakdown is evidence of the successful realization of the goals, values, and perspectives of the industrial era. What is important now is to respond creatively and to find a new beginning—a fresh start with a revitalized sense of civilizational purpose.

There is no one to blame for our movement into a stage of civilizational transition. Who can be blamed when the problems we face are intrinsic to the intertwined structure of life in which we all participate? The views and values that arose in realizing the potentials of the industrial era were fitting for that time. Now these same views and values are becoming increasingly ill suited for carrying us into the future. Although no one is to blame, we are all responsible for where we go from here.

We can put our predicament into perspective by turning, once again, to the work of the historian Arnold Toynbee. After analyzing the dynamics of development of all the major civilizations throughout history, he concluded that a civilization will begin to disintegrate when it loses its capacity to respond creatively to major challenges. Toynbee also concluded that *a failure of creativity often follows a period of great civilizational achievement.* When we consider industrialized nations and their two centuries of unparalleled material achievement, we should be especially wary of social complacency and diminished creativity. After acquiring a civilizational self-image of seemingly invincible mastery, many devel-

oped nations find themselves in the demoralizing position of being unable to manage their own affairs, let
alone cope creatively with mounting global problems. It
is time to seek out fresh approaches to national and
global challenges rather than to redouble efforts along
old lines.

Toynbee was clear in stating that a civilization is not
bound to succumb when it enters a stage of breakdown.
Particularly in a democratic society, when a civilization
fails to employ its inventive capacity and begins to disintegrate, then it is the people themselves who bear ultimate responsibility. Movement into a condition of
traumatic breakdown is not inevitable unless citizens
collectively acquiesce, through complacency and inac-
tion, to that outcome.

The Pace of Civilizational Transition

How long might it take to reach either a condition
of devastating breakdown or to accomplish a creative
breakthrough that leads to a new era of sustainable,
global development? This is impossible to predict with
accuracy. Although I have used a smooth curve to portray movement through the four stages of growth, I do
not think our journey down the backside of the development curve will be this smooth. Just as our ride up

the front side of this developmental curve had many bumps, plateaus, and sudden jumps, so, too, will similar variation characterize our movement through the systems-breakdown region of development. Although it is impossible to predict with precision when a majority of industrialized nations might reach a condition of breakdown or initial breakthrough, still, this is such an important concern that I would like to venture a rough estimate of timing. As mentioned in the opening chapter, a number of trends involving population, resources, and the environment will become critical by the second decade of the twenty-first century. Therefore my best guess is that industrialized nations will be forced to confront squarely the challenge of civilizational disintegration or revitalization no later than the 2020s. This does *not* mean the situation will be resolved; rather it means that by this time we will find whether we are up to the challenge of responding fully and wholeheartedly to a world that is in a profound crisis.

Given the long lead time required to invent and implement new ways of living and working that are essential for a sustainable future, the hour is already late— our situation is already critical. As precious years slip by, our range of options narrows drastically. An unavoidable task for many who are alive today will be to begin reinventing and re-creating our way of living on the planet.

The Challenge of Reconciliation and Transition

I do not view the stage of "systems breakdown" as a time of abrupt and apocalyptic change. Instead, the wintertime of the industrial era seems likely to be characterized by an extended period of disharmony, discord, and fragmentation. Given a biosphere already stretched past its ability to carry the burden of humanity, nations around the world will be squeezed increasingly by unyielding limits to growth. Despite the severity of our problems, I do not expect the productive capacity of industrial nations to be destroyed. Indeed, outward physical appearances could suggest that nothing so momentous as a global transformation is in fact happening. *The most fundamental challenge that arises in the season of systems breakdown is an invisible crisis: a loss of social cohesion around a compelling civilizational purpose that mobilizes our collective efforts and draws out our enthusiastic participation in life.*

We humans can bear many hardships when the burden feels meaningful. However, without a compelling sense of social purpose, feelings of futility and despair begin to permeate our lives. Without a sense of meaningful participation in life, we lose our bearings, begin to wander, and become disoriented. *An overriding challenge in the winter of civilizational growth is to find a new "common sense"—a new sense of reality, human identity, and social purpose that we can hold in common and that respects our radically changing global circumstances.* Finding this new common sense in the middle of the turbulence and disarray of the breakdown of industrial civilizations is likely to be a drawn-out, messy, and ambiguous process of social learning. How effectively we use our tools of mass communication to achieve a new consensus will be critical in determining the ultimate outcome of this season of growth.

I do not expect a quick or easy resolution to the difficult conditions of the stage of systems breakdown. Only after people express their anger and sadness over the broken dreams of material prosperity will they turn to the task of building a sustainable economy. Only after people communicate their despair that we may never be able to restore the integrity of the global ecology will we work wholeheartedly for its renewal. Only after people express their unwillingness to make material sacrifices unless their actions are matched fairly by others will a majority of people begin to live in a more ecologically sound manner. Only after people have exhausted the hope that the golden era of industrial growth can somehow be revived will we collectively venture forward. We are moving into a traumatic time of social turmoil that will either transform—or devastate—the very soul of industrial cultures.

Although there are many reasons to resist change, if we (as individuals) fail to begin our grass-roots adaptation to the profoundly changing global circumstances, we (as societies) will be ill prepared when the full force of the global challenge hits us. Then the social fabric of nations could be torn apart violently, democracy could dissolve, and anarchy or, more likely, an authoritarian government could take its place. There are no quick fixes—technological or psychological—to remedy our situation. I think we will be several decades into the twenty-first century before we pass through this dark night in our life cycle and emerge again in an awakening springtime of civilizational development with a renewed sense of purpose.

THREE OUTCOMES FROM A PERIOD OF CIVILIZATIONAL BREAKDOWN

Three outcomes seem to encompass the possible alternatives most likely to emerge from our stage of systems breakdown. One outcome is the *collapse* of civilizations as the biosphere is pushed beyond its ability to support the burden of humanity and suffers crippling devastation. A second outcome is the *stagnation* of civilizations as people and nations expend all of their energy and creativity in simply maintaining the status quo. A third outcome is a *revitalizing* world civilization that emerges from a period of intense communication and reconciliation that builds a working consensus around a sustainable pathway into the future. These three pathways are summarized below:

Three Pathways into the Future

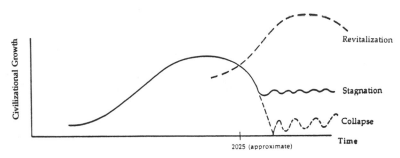

- **Revitalization.** People embrace challenges; a time of compressed social invention and creativity
- **Stagnation.** People retreat from challenges and seek security in a highly managed social order
- **Collapse.** People ignore challenges; the biosphere collapses and causes a massive die-off of humans and other species of life, both plant and animal
- **Civilizational Breakdown.** The winter of industrial civilizations and a crisis of transition; the traditional view of the world is depleted and a workable alternative is not yet in place

There are unique dynamics that will move civilizations toward one outcome or another. Here are three scenarios that suggest how we could evolve into each one of these futures.

Future I—Overshoot and Collapse

A range of psychological attitudes produce delays in responding to the ecological crisis, and this results in the overshoot and collapse of the earth's carrying capacity. Instead of rising to the challenge of sustainability, a majority of persons respond with:

- *Denial*—Some insist this is not a time of fundamental civilizational transition, and that current
  distress is merely a short-term aberration, and
  that things will soon return to "normal."

- *Helplessness*—Others feel helpless to make a difference and simultaneously assume that someone
  else must be in control, so they do not get involved. In feeling powerless to do anything constructive, people adopt a posture of fatalistic
  resignation toward what appears to be an unstoppable process of disintegration.

- *Blame*—Others assume that some ethnic group,
  nation, religion, or political group is to blame for
  these problems, so they invest their creative energy
  in looking for various scapegoats.

- *Escape*—Others acknowledge the seriousness of
  the situation and look for ways in which they and
  their friends can escape from a disintegrating situation; some seek to live in self-sufficiency in isolated rural areas, while the wealthy search for
  secure enclaves in which to "ride out the storm."

In this scenario the mass media, particularly television, are a powerful force in promoting ecological
collapse. By aggressively promoting a consumerist consciousness in order to sell advertising, the mass media
dampen public concern and divert public attention from

urgent global challenges. By masking the reality of the world situation and generating a false sense of normalcy that ignores critical issues, the mass media retard the process of social learning. Democratic processes falter and fail as an ill-informed and ill-prepared citizenry loses the race with the intertwined pattern of problems that are growing rapidly in complexity and severity.

With delay the grass-roots organizations that might have brought an infusion of creativity and innovation into the situation are too few and too weak to make a substantial difference. As a result, people are forced to rely almost exclusively on aging and inflexible bureaucracies that themselves have reached their limits to cope with problems of enormous scale and complexity. With no larger vision beyond that of sheer survival, people and institutions try only to hold on to traditional ways of living. With most nations adopting a lifeboat ethic and turning away from responsibilities to the overall biosphere and human family, the world begins a nearly unstoppable slide into calamity.

By responding with too little and too late, the intertwined array of problems (overpopulation, resource depletion, environmental pollution, species extinction, climate change, etc.) exacerbate one another and grow rapidly to devastating proportions. Then, like a rubber band stretched beyond the limits of its elasticity, the global ecology is pushed past its capacity for self-repair and fragments catastrophically. With the global ecology and economy devastated, fierce wars over access to resources (water, farmland, oil, forests, etc.) result, thereby undermining the remaining trust and goodwill essential for working cooperatively to build a sustainable future. Life then degenerates into a survivalist nightmare where the primary concern for most people is the security of their immediate family and friends. The diminished sense of social responsibility of the survivalist orientation accelerates the destruction of the biosphere and produces a downward spiral of war and environmental devastation that feeds upon itself. Within a generation or two the biosphere becomes so crippled, and the people of the planet so divided by conflict, that a new dark age develops. For the foreseeable future there is neither the social nor the ecological foundation upon which to rebuild human civilization.

Future II—Dynamic Stagnation

A future of dynamic stagnation emerges when a society is unwilling to make the creative leap forward and instead expends all of its energy trying to perpetuate the status quo and keep from falling backward. Although there is not sufficient vision and creativity to transform the situation, citizens make such persistent and determined efforts to cope that the end result is a dynamic stalemate between the forces of advance and the forces of collapse. By redoubling efforts along lines that worked well in the past, societies are able to maintain themselves, but they are not able to surpass themselves—and the outcome is dynamic stagnation.

A wide range of risky technological interventions are employed in an effort to cope with the deteriorating world situation: growing reliance upon nuclear power (with all of the attendant concerns for pollution and safety); heavy reliance upon bioengineering for new sources of food that are, for example, resistant to ozone depletion, acid rains, drought, and so on; the genetic engineering of humans to cope with the consequences of damage to DNA and outbreaks of cancer caused by pollution; reliance upon computerized monitoring of people and organizations thought to be a threat to an increasingly interdependent economy (with its vulnerable energy grids, computer networks, transportation systems, etc.).

Although citizens in developed nations are willing to make modest concessions to equity and fairness in the distribution of the world's resources, it is only enough to prevent the collapse of the global economic and social system, and it is not sufficient to transform the world's economy into a synergistic process of mutually supportive development. Developed nations continue to spend a significant share of scarce national resources on their military to protect their wealth from the growing demands of the world's poor for a more equitable use of resources and productive capacity. These minimal concessions keep the developing world simmering just below the threshold of revolution.

Instead of developing new institutional structures more adapted to changing circumstances (for example, a strong United Nations at the global scale and strong eco-villages at the neighborhood scale), people depend on traditional bureaucracies, despite their growing rigidity and authoritarian tendencies. To prevent social collapse in the face of extreme ecological and economic stress, a highly managed society emerges that imposes stability and order on the situation. Many historic freedoms, both political and economic, are suspended as massive and deadening bureaucracies attempt to manage many facets of life. Though well-meaning, these bureaucracies preempt local initiative and raise the level of dependency on remote centers of power. As people turn to paternalistic institutions to manage social affairs that they think they are unable to manage for themselves, the vitality of the social order is strangled in a web of bureaucracy. The threat of social chaos has been replaced with predictability, order, and security; however, the will and creativity of civilizations is ensnared in a complex maze of bureaucracy and regulation.

In many urban areas, the "city boss" form of leadership again becomes commonplace, turning many cities into virtual fiefdoms. Affluent communities are turned into mini–police states as they hire private forces to protect their property from the increasingly desperate and resentful poor. Government surveillance of persons and groups who threaten law and order is widespread. In this fearful and somber setting, people and organizations are under constant scrutiny. Secret information banks blossom with financial, political, medical, religious, and other information. Guerrilla warfare, using computer viruses and other forms of electronic sabotage, is common as individuals and groups attempt to destroy or cripple these information banks. The mass media are restricted in the scope and content of programming. Most of the global communication networks are controlled by a few antagonistic coalitions of nation-states and international corporations.

As everyone struggles desperately to hold on, the whole social order sinks ever deeper into psychological malaise and a bureaucratic stranglehold. There is much "sound and fury signifying nothing"—we are at war with ourselves and our fear of the unknown challenges that lie beyond the industrial era. For most people this is a highly stressful future in which living is little more than "only not dying."

The way that a nation could sink into a condition of stagnation is illustrated by an infamous laboratory experiment. A frog was placed in a beaker of boiling water and, not surprisingly, promptly jumped out. Then the frog was placed in a beaker of cold water that was slowly warmed to boiling temperature. The change in temperature was sufficiently gradual that the frog adapted in increments, making no attempt to escape. By the time he instinctively realized the danger, it was too late. Weakened, he could no longer jump out—so he died. In a similar process of adaptation the creativity and initiative of people could be drained, increment by increment, in deadening bureaucracies. Few would consciously choose such an outcome. Therefore arrested growth will emerge, not from conscious choice, but from unconscious acquiescence to the seemingly rational dictates for coping with growing national and global crises.

Future III—Reconciliation and Revitalization

A sustainable future emerges when citizens recognize the absolute necessity of change and use their tools of mass communication to undertake an unprecedented level of dialogue about the most healthy pathway ahead. With ongoing, local-to-global communication comes mutual understanding and gradual reconciliation around a shared vision of a sustainable future. With an overarching vision held in common and a commitment to realizing that vision, the human family makes dramatic reductions in military expenditures, begins to heal the global ecology, makes development investments in poorer nations, builds new energy systems, and in many other ways begins to build a promising future.

To build a sustainable future, citizens of the earth must see themselves as part of a tightly interdependent system rather than as isolated individuals and nations. With a witnessing consciousness or observer's perspective, citizens cultivate the detachment that enables us to stand back, look at the big picture, and make the hard choices and trade-offs that our circumstances demand. With a reflective consciousness we look at our situation objectively and see how imperative it is to begin the process of healing and reconciliation.

The communications revolution plays a critical role in global consciousness raising and consensus building. With the rapid development of sophisticated communication networks, the global consciousness of humanity awakens decisively. The integration of computers, telephones, television, satellites, and fiber optics into a unified, interactive multimedia system gives the world a powerful voice, and a palpable conscience. The earth has a new vehicle for its collective thinking and invention that transcends any nation or culture. From this communications revolution comes a trailblazing, new level of human creativity, daring, and action in response to the global ecological crisis.

The mass media are used in several ways to function as a sophisticated tool for active social learning and decision making. First, whole new areas and forms of television programming emerge; for example, entire channels are devoted to exploring alternative ways of living and working. Second, the lateral conversation of democracy—citizen-to-citizen dialogue—explodes into an unprecedented level of social communication and consensus building at every level—local, national, and global. Third, the interaction between an informed citizenry and their leaders in government also blossoms. Rather than feeling cynical or powerless, citizens feel engaged and responsible for society and its future. Democratic processes are revitalized as citizens are empowered to cope with mounting crises and to participate in decision making. With a free and open exchange of information and visions, and with safeguards to prevent any one group or nation from dominating the conversation of democracy, a foundation for building a sustainable future is firmly established.

A revitalizing society is a decentralizing society, with grass-roots organizations that are numerous enough, have arisen soon enough, and are effective enough to provide a genuine alternative to more centralized bureaucracies. These organizations are taking charge of activities that formerly were handled by state and federal agencies: education, housing, crime prevention, child care, health care, job training, and so on. The strength and resiliency of the social fabric grows as local organizations promote self-help, self-organization, a community spirit, and neighborhood bonding. With control over many of life's basic activities brought back to the local level, a strong foundation is established to compensate for faltering bureaucracies at the state and federal level.

By breaking the cultural hypnosis of consumerism, developing ecological ways of living, building more conscious and engaged democracies, using the mass media as a potent tool for active social learning, and developing grass roots organizations, a new cultural consensus emerges rapidly. Industrialized nations move beyond the historic agenda of self-serving material progress to a new, life-serving agenda of promoting the well-being of the entire human family. Despite enormous economic, ecological, and social stresses, an overarching vision of a sustainable and satisfying future provides sufficient social glue to hold humanity together while working through these trying times. A new sense of global community, human dignity, goodwill, and trust is growing. Although problems still abound, it is clear that a new springtime of development is emerging.

Three great paths lie before us. They overlap at present, but diverge increasingly as we move into the future. Both our personal choices and our collective communication will be critical in determining where we go from here:

- We get *collapse* by perpetuating the status quo and running the biosphere into ruin.
- We get *stagnation* when citizens are passive and

rely upon remote bureaucracies and technological solutions to handle a deteriorating local-to-global situation.

- We get *revitalization* only when we directly engage our predicament as individuals, families, communities, and nations.

A progression is evident—the most favorable outcome depends directly upon individuals and families making a strong commitment to grass-roots involvement.

THE GLOBAL DIMENSIONS OF CHANGE

Our time of wrenching transition is not restricted to industrialized nations—virtually all of the world's civilizations have entered a time of profound change. It seems no accident that the very time when the human family finds itself shoulder to shoulder in an interdependent and vulnerable world is also the time when civilizations are breaking down and transforming. The social, economic, and ecological stresses of our times are evidence of the progress of birth—the labor pains of a global civilization and consciousness are being felt. The process of civilizational breakdown is necessary for building a sustainable future. The human family cannot open itself to the possibility of a global community while doggedly fixed to social structures and a view of the world that no longer matches our situation.

We are moving toward some form of global community and consciousness at breathtaking speed. The challenges we face—economic, ecological, cultural, and political—are part of a tightly intertwined network of global activity. We must adopt an approach and perspective that is equal in scope to the problems we face. The human family is now obliged to discover a global vision of a sustainable future that honors human unity while fostering human diversity.

Although humanity confronts a critical time of transition, the importance of this should not be inflated unduly. In one respect, it is simply one more link in a long chain of human evolution. The present era is no more important than any other—failure to forge a strong link anywhere along the chain will weaken the entire structure of development. Yet, in another respect, the now-emerging link in our civilizational chain that leads to some form of planetary consciousness and consensus seems particularly vital. If we can open to reciprocal learning with other cultures and, through that learning, find a shared sense of reality, human identity, and social purpose that draws out our enthusiasm for life, then I think the evolution of humanity will lead in presently unanticipated directions and to unforeseen heights.

In the past the idea of a peaceful and mutually supportive global civilization was viewed as a utopian dream. Now, it is a requirement for continuing human evolution. If we do not rise to this challenge, we will surely unleash upon ourselves the most massive wave of suffering ever experienced in human history. Time has run out. The era of creative adaptation is already upon us.

CHOOSING OUR FUTURE

Three great alternatives lie ahead—collapse, stagnation, or transformation. They overlap at present but will increasingly diverge as we move into the future. The dimensions of change that are now occurring are extraordinary. Like giant icebergs breaking loose from ancient moorings and beginning to float free for the first time in hundreds, even thousands, of years, entire civilization's are melting, moving, and changing. We have begun a process of transition that extends from the individual to the global scale.

We are not alone in this time of change. Everyone we meet is in some way involved with his or her own personal struggle to respond to our time of challenge. Whatever our other differences may be, we are all participants in this historical rite of passage.

As individuals we are not powerless in the face of this monumental change. Opportunities for meaningful and important action are everywhere: the food we eat, the work we do, the transportation we use, the manner in which we relate to others, the clothing we wear, the learning we acquire, the compassionate causes we support, the level of attention we invest in our moment-to-moment passage through life, and so on. The list is endless, since the stuff of social transformation is identical with the stuff from which our daily lives are constructed.

We are each responsible for the conduct of our lives—and we are each unique. Therefore we are each uniquely responsible for our actions and choices in this pivotal time in human evolution. There is no one who can take our place. We each weave a singular strand in the web of life. No one else can weave that strand for us. What we each contribute is distinct, and what we each withhold is uniquely irreplaceable.

More than anything else, the outcome from this time of planetary transition will depend on the choices that we make as individuals. There are no preconditions to our choosing a revitalizing path of civilizational development. There is nothing lacking. Nothing more is needed than what we already have. We require no remarkable, undiscovered technologies. We do not need heroic, larger-than-life leadership. The *only* requirement is that we, as individuals, choose a revitalizing future and then work in community with others to bring it to fruition. By our conscious choices we can move from alienation to community, from despair to creativity, from passivity to participation, from stagnation to learning, from cynicism to caring. We tend to think that we are powerless, helpless, impotent. Yet the reality is that only we—as individuals working in cooperation with one another—have the power to transform our situation. Far from being helpless, we are the only source from which the necessary creativity, compassion, and will can arise. The time of civilizational challenge is already upon us. The autumn of the industrial era of development has already moved into winter. It is time to begin the next stage of our human journey.

Chapter Seven

Chapter Seven

⋇

CIVILIZATIONAL

REVITALIZATION

SIMPLICITY OF LIVING IS ESSENTIAL IF WE ARE TO AVOID the evolutionary detours of either ecological collapse or bureaucratic stagnation and instead create a sustainable and satisfying future for humanity. Reiterating a key insight from the introduction, Arnold Toynbee summarized a lifetime of study of the nature of civilizational growth with his Law of Progressive Simplification. This law asserts that as evolution proceeds, a civilization will transfer increasing increments of energy and attention from the material to the nonmaterial side of life and that this will be expressed through developing culture (music, art, drama, literature) and a growing capacity for compassion, caring community, and self-governance. A progressively simpler way of living, then, is not only essential for responding to the ecological crisis (maintaining ourselves), it is also a vital expression of an evolving civilization (surpassing ourselves).

Despite the need for and evolutionary promise of simpler living, embracing this life-way represents an enormously demanding undertaking for developed nations. A level of social consciousness, consensus, and commitment is required from millions of persons that has never before existed in human history. Were it not for the push of unyielding necessity, few people would choose this path. Yet because necessity is the mother of invention, we now need to become skilled midwives to aid in the birth of an array of social, economic, and political inventions that are essential if we are to respond to our time of growing urgency.

Two major areas of change are addressed in this chapter—illustrative material changes that support a revitalizing civilization and major nonmaterial changes that need to accompany these substantive changes. The latter includes: (a) reorienting of the mass media to break the cultural hypnosis of consumerism; (b) promoting a more conscious democracy that involves citizens in making choices for the future; (c) fostering reconciliation among the many polarities that now divide humanity; and (d) developing positive images of a sustainable future.

MATERIAL CHANGES SUPPORTIVE OF A REVITALIZING CIVILIZATION

A wide range of changes will characterize industrial societies that are moving toward more ecological approaches to living; for example:

- Energy conservation would become widespread and involve, for example, fuel-efficient autos, the insulation and redesign of homes to allow maximum use of passive solar heating, the use of photovoltaic sources, and so on. Overall, industrial societies would begin to turn away from the "hard energy path" of reliance on imported oil, coal, and nuclear power and instead move toward a "soft energy path" that emphasizes conservation, solar power, and the use of renewable energy sources (such as biomass, geothermal, and wave and wind power). Coupled with these changes would be much more extensive use of electronic communication or "telecommuting" as a substitute for physical travel. Greater use would also be made of energy-efficient modes of transportation (car pools, buses, trains, bicycles).

- Economic growth would become much more selective or differentiated: some sectors of the economy would be contracting (especially those that are wasteful of energy and oriented toward conspicuous consumption), while other sectors would be expanding (for example, information processing, interactive communications, intensive agriculture, retrofitting homes and cities for energy efficiency, education, etc.) To minimize the costs of transportation and distribution in an energy-scarce setting, markets would be more decentralized and localized. People would buy more goods and services from local producers, and this in turn would lead to a rebirth of entrepreneurial activity at the local level. Small businesses that are well adapted to local conditions and local needs would flourish. New types of markets and marketplaces would proliferate—flea markets, community markets, and extensive bartering networks (whose efficiency will be greatly enhanced by new generations of computers that match goods and services with potential consumers/traders). The economy would also become more democratized as workers take a larger role in decision making.

•

People would change their patterns of consumption in favor of products that are functional, durable, energy efficient, nonpolluting, easily repairable, healthy, and produced by ethical firms. A consumerist orientation would grow as people boycott goods and services sold by firms whose policies are considered unethical or unsound with regard to the environment, fairness to workers, overseas investment policy, and so on.

- Voluntary changes in consumption patterns would be reinforced by making changes in the tax structure; for example, placing higher taxes on the wealthy, luxury goods, gasoline, alcohol, and cigarettes. These tax revenues would then be used to provide enhanced health-care services, expanded education, renewable-energy programs, and so on. Tax cuts would be given to those that, for example, retrofit homes and apartments for sustainability by installing passive solar heating, better insulation, and so on. These changes in the tax structure would be reinforced through "ecological advertising" that promotes a concern for the well-being of the earth.

- Massive investments would be made in cleaning up the polluted land, air, and water. Much emphasis would be placed on designing new generations of industrial processes that minimize pollution and maximize recycling.

- There would be rapid growth in the number of classes, videos, computer services, publications, and so forth dealing with do-it-yourself activities ranging from home construction and repair to cooking and gardening. Overall there would be a rebirth in the sense of personal competence and craftsmanship.

• Civic involvement would be greatly increased through both voluntary and mandatory programs. A new era of volunteerism would blossom as people work with disadvantaged youth, urban-renewal projects, programs to assist developing nations, and so on. A year or more of national service could become mandatory for young people and could involve work ranging from building community centers and helping clean up the environment to restoring historical sites.

• There would be a rebirth in the importance of the local neighborhood and community as an area of work, play, and mutually helpful living. The number of eco-villages or microcommunities would proliferate and contain a diverse range of activities; for example, neighborhood workplaces (perhaps a telecommuting center or crafts center or child-care center, etc.), community gardens, recycling centers, food cooperatives, neighborhood schools, and so on. Urban land that was formerly used for lawns and flower gardens would be used increasingly for supplemental food sources (vegetable gardens, fruit and nut trees) and as a part of the community commons. These neighborhood-sized "villages" would have the flavor and

cohesiveness of a small town and the sophistica-
tion of a larger city as they would be nestled
within a communications-rich urban setting. In
addition to technical and architectural innovations, there would be accompanying changes in
zoning laws, building codes, financing methods,
and ownership arrangements to support the de
velopment of new forms of housing.

The foregoing list only begins to suggest the practical, down-to-earth adaptations that would characterize
a revitalizing civilization. This illustrative sampling of
changes shows that adopting ecological modes of living
does not mean a return to a more primitive past but
movement ahead to a more sophisticated, compassionate, and cooperative future.

Breaking the Cultural Hypnosis of Consumerism

To build a sustainable future will require dramatic
changes in the overall levels and patterns of consumption
in developed nations. To change consumption levels and
patterns will require a new consciousness and new consensus among millions of persons—and this will require
dramatic changes in the consumerist messages we give
ourselves through the mass media, particularly televi-

sion. In the United States 98 percent of all homes have a TV set, and the average person watches more than four hours of television per day. In addition, a majority of people get a majority of their news from this source. What is more, the average person will see more than 35,000 commercials each year. Television is more powerful than either the schools or the workplace in creating our shared view of reality and social identity. Not surprisingly, then, television is the most powerful instrument in developed nations for promoting either consumption or conservation.

Currently, the television industry is aggressively promoting high-consumption lifestyles and ignoring the redefinition of the "good life" that is needed if we are to build a more sustainable future. The television industry is understandably unsympathetic to simpler ways of living. Television stations make their profits by delivering the largest possible audience of potential consumers to corporate advertisers. Mass entertainment is used to capture the attention of a mass audience that is then appealed to by mass advertising in order to promote mass consumption. The television industry deliberately ignores the views and values of those who have little to spend (the poor) and those who choose to spend little (the frugal person or family that is more concerned with the quality of being than the quantity of having).

The profound consumerist bias of contemporary television creates an impossible double bind: People use the consumption levels and patterns portrayed in TV advertising to evaluate their levels of personal well-being while those same consumption patterns are simultaneously devastating the environment and resource base on which our future depends. If the old adage that "one picture is worth a thousand words" is correct, then the 35,000 or so commercials that people see each year represent the equivalent of 35 million words (!) about the seeming importance of material consumption to our happiness and satisfaction with life. These commercials are far more than a pitch for a particular product—they are also advertisements for the attitudes, values, and lifestyles that surround consumption of that product. The clothing, cars, settings, and other elements that create the context for an advertisement send strong, implicit messages as to the standards of living and patterns of behavior that are the norm for society. Not surprisingly, more frugal patterns of living and consuming seldom appear on television. These themes would threaten the legitimacy and potency of the television-induced cultural hypnosis generated by a self-perpetuating cycle of mass entertainment, mass advertising, and mass consumption. By default, industrial societies are left with programming and advertising that selectively portray and powerfully reinforce a materialistic orientation toward life. *By programming television to achieve commercial success, the mind-set of entire nations is being programmed for ecological failure.*

The most precious resource of a civilization—the shared consciousness of its citizenry—is literally being prostituted and sold to the highest corporate bidders. Each day we are putting our collective values, attitudes, and priorities up for sale. The pervasive commercialization of television (and thus society) represents far more than an offense to "good taste"—it is crippling our capacity to comprehend and respond to the mounting ecological crisis. Commercialization is distorting and undermining the very foundation of civilization—the view of reality and social identity that we hold in common. Television advertising takes exceedingly trivial concerns (such as which deodorant, shampoo, or denture adhesive to use) and blows them up into issues of seemingly enormous importance for our lives. Concerns that are utterly insignificant relative to the task of making it through this time of profound ecological and social transition are given vastly inflated significance and then force-fed into our collective consciousness. *To break the cultural hypnosis of consumerism, we must begin by breaking the corporate stranglehold on television!*

The point is not to condemn all television advertising and entertainment; rather, it is to acknowledge the great need for balance in our diet of images and information so that we can choose a healthy approach to consumption. Because we require a new level of maturity as consumers, we also require a new level of responsibility in how we use television. Three major changes in how we use television are essential for a revitalizing civilization:

First, we need ecologically oriented advertising to balance the onslaught of proconsumerist messages and to foster a mind-set of authentic choice in our consumption behavior. To balance the psychological impact of the one-sided avalanche of commercials, we need "ecological ads" that encourage people to consume with an appreciation of their impact on the world's dwindling resources and deteriorating environment.

Second, because television teaches continuously about the lifestyles and values that are the "norm" for society, we need entertainment programming that actively explores issues of sustainability as well as simpler lifestyles. Television teaches by what it ignores as well as by what it addresses. If an ecological consciousness and an ethic of frugality are missing from entertainment programming, then they are likely to be missing from our cultural consciousness as well. We need entertainment programming that explores ecological concerns, alternative ways of living, and innovative role models.

Third, we need expanded documentaries and investigative reports describing, in depth, the global challenges we now face. Because the overwhelming majority of prime-time hours on television are devoted to entertainment programming, we are entertainment rich and knowledge poor. Our situation is like that of a long-distance runner who prepares for a marathon by eating primarily junk food. We are filling our social brain with a diet of entertainment at the very time our democracies face problems of marathon proportions. We are trivial-izing our civilizational consciousness at the very time we need robust communication about our pathway into the future. This is a recipe for disaster. We need a quantum increase in the level of ecologically relevant program-ming and a new social commitment to strong investi-gative reporting that awakens public concern around issues of sustainability.

These proposals will surely face opposition from TV stations and advertisers who fear their profits will be di-minished by an ecological consciousness. It is not by acci-dent that *the last taboo topic on television is television itself* and how it is being used to promote the psychology of mass consumption and how this psychology, in turn, threatens the future of our species and the planet. The responsibility for change lies not so much with the tele-vision industry but with ourselves as individual citizens. Our use of television is so integral to our civilizational consciousness that the entire use of this medium must become a major social issue worthy of sustained and searching debate by all members of society.

CONSCIOUS DEMOCRACY

Communication is the lifeblood of democracy. To actively choose a sustainable future, citizens need to be able to communicate among themselves so that together they can bring that future into being. We need a "conscious democracy," one that pays attention to what is going on and that uses the modern tools of mass communication to enable citizens to engage in an unprecedented new level of dialogue and consensus building about the future. A healthy democracy requires the active consent of the governed, not simply their passive acquiescence. Therefore we need to move beyond using television as a one-way, passive medium and begin using it in conjunction with telephones and computers to create a two-way or interactive medium for citizen learning and dialogue.

Democracy has often been called the art of the possible. If we don't know how our fellow citizens think and feel about policies to create a sustainable future, then we float powerless in a sea of ambiguity and are unable to mobilize ourselves into constructive action. The most powerful and direct way to revitalize democracy is by improving the ability of citizens to know their own minds as an overall community, region, or nation. Trust in the good judgment of citizens seems well founded. For example, after a half century of polling U.S. public opinion, George Gallup concluded that the collective judgment of citizens was "extraordinarily sound."[1] He also said that citizens are often ahead of their elected leaders in accepting innovations and radical changes.

Given that we can trust the collective wisdom of the body politic, we need to cultivate that wisdom by engaging in regular "electronic town meetings" at every scale—local, national, and global. By combining televised dialogues on key issues with near instantaneous feedback from a scientific sample of citizens, the public can know its collective sentiments with a high degree of accuracy. Just as a doctor can take a very small sample of blood and obtain an accurate picture of the overall condition of one's body, so, too, can a relatively small, random sample of citizens be used to get a reliable picture of the strength, texture, and intensity of the views of the overall body politic.

With regular electronic town meetings (combined with other types of forums), the perspectives and priorities of the citizenry could be rapidly brought into public view and the democratic process revitalized. When a working consensus emerges, it would presumably guide (but not compel) decision makers. The value of electronic town meetings is *not* as a vehicle for citizens to attempt to micromanage government through direct democracy; rather, its value is as a vehicle for citizens to discover their widely shared priorities that can guide their representatives in government. Involving citizens in choosing the pathway into the future will not guarantee that the "right" choices will always be made, but it will guarantee that citizens will feel involved and invested in those choices. Rather than feeling cynical and powerless, citizens will feel engaged and responsible for our future.

One of the biggest challenges humanity now faces is to evolve the art and practice of conscious democracy in the communications era. To realize this challenge, we cannot rely upon government agencies and media corporations—these institutions are perpetuating the status quo. What is needed is a grass-roots social movement focused on the ecologically responsible uses of the mass media. Just as the environmental movement, feminist movement, and civil rights movement emerged from the grass roots, we require a citizen-based, "communication rights" movement that seeks a fair and just use of our tools of mass communication in service of a sustainable future for humanity. Each generation must renew its commitment to democracy in ways that respect the unique demands of the times. In this generation, our contract with democracy requires citizens to confront the unprecedented challenge of developing the tools and skills for mass social dialogue and consensus building that respond to the needs for building a sustainable future.

GLOBAL RECONCILIATION

Humanity is profoundly divided: between the rich and the poor, between racial groups, between ethnic groups, between religious groups, between men and women, between current and future generations, between humans and other species, between geographic regions, and many more. If humanity is to work together cooperatively to build a sustainable future, we must learn to bridge these differences and to build an integrated global community. Without reconciliation, efforts to achieve a sustainable future will be stalemated and blocked by conflict—and humanity will descend into a new dark age marked by chronic warfare, ecological collapse, and great misery.

At the heart of the challenge of reconciliation is the need to bring legitimate grievances into the healing light of public awareness, to take responsibility for them, and to seek just remedies. Reconciliation does not mean that the injustices of the past will be forgotten and erased; rather, it means they will not stand in the way of our collective progress into the future.

We are in an unyielding race between global reconciliation and unimaginable calamity. Because virtually all of the world's critical challenges are human-caused, they are fundamentally communication problems. We need to employ the powerful tools of mass communication now blossoming around the world to achieve the level of understanding and reconciliation essential for building a sustainable future. With communication we have a realistic opportunity to acknowledge and work through the many divisions that now exist.

To achieve authentic and lasting reconciliation, we need to affirm compassion as a practical basis for organizing human affairs. To see the down-to-earth role of compassion, consider three different foundations for a global social order: force, law, and love.

If *force* is the foundation for planetary civilization, then it will likely produce either global domination by a single superpower or unstable competition between blocks of nations. Because a militaristic culture would honor neither our human unity nor tolerate much in the way of diversity, it would greatly limit human freedoms and creativity. Living would then truly be little more than "only not dying." Gandhi often spoke about the wasteful detour in human evolution that results when we depend on violence to solve our difficulties as nations. He said this "law of the jungle" behavior was fitting for the consciousness of animals, but for we humans to conduct our lives in this manner was to turn away from our higher potentials and to reverse the course of evolution.[2] If force is the foundation for a global social order, we will be moving back into the darkness of human conflict and suffering from which we have struggled so mightily to free ourselves.

A second foundation for global civilization is *law*. By this I mean that the human family could establish formal rules of conduct that would allow people and nations to relate with a minimum of forceful coercion. For a legalistic foundation for a global community to be effective, some democratically constituted body such as the United Nations would have to take a much stronger role in international relations. The responsibilities of the United Nations would likely include peacekeeping as well as ensuring the minimal well-being of persons and the planet with regard to food, health, energy, and the environment. Conflict would still persist, but the most destructive forms of warfare would be eliminated.

It is appropriate that we have a mistrust of a legal-istic—and therefore bureaucratic—basis for maintain-ing a global community. When we consider the nature and scope of bureaucracy needed to enforce a legalistic basis for human affairs, then it seems quite plausible that the eventual outcome would be a suffocating bu-reaucracy of planetary scope. At the same time that law might liberate humanity from the threat of physical warfare, it could strangle our creativity in a vast web of bureaucracy and greatly inhibit the vitality of evo-lution.

A third foundation for global community is *com-passion*. The word *passion* means "to suffer," and the word *compassion* literally means "to be with suffering." If we open ourselves to the unadorned experience of just being in the world with all of its suffering, we are relating to the world with compassion. The very act of experi-encing the world as it already is—directly and without sentiment or pretense—is to experience the world compassionately. To relate to the world compassionately is to know the world accurately. With compassion as the foundation for international relations, we will tend to touch the world more lightly and gently with our bureaucracies, and we will tend to honor human unity while tolerating (or even encouraging) human diversity.

Compassion is a realistic foundation for human relations as it is a part of the "common sense" of humanity. Although this common sense may be variously stated, it is widely recognized:

Christianity:
"As you wish that men would do to you, do so to them."
—Luke 6:31

Buddhism:
"Hurt not others in ways that you yourself would find hurtful."
—Udanavarga

Judaism:
"That which is hateful unto you, do not impose on others."
—Talmud, Shabbat 31a

Hinduism:
"Do naught unto others which would cause you pain if done to you."
—Mahabharata 5:1517

Islam:
"No one of you is a believer until he desires for his brother that which he desires for himself."
—Sunan

Confucianism:
"Do not unto others what you would not have them do unto you."
—Analects 15:23

These affirmations of a "golden rule" are like different facets of a single jewel or like different branches of a single tree. At some level the human family already recognizes the immense practical value of compassion as a basis for human affairs. Many people recognize that in weakening others we are weakening ourselves. Many also understand that the human family will need all its strength if it is successfully to negotiate this time of planetary transition.

Acting in a compassionate manner that is life-sensing and life-serving is not a spiritual platitude divorced from the hard realities of life. If one corporate officer were to choose to shift from a self-serving to a life-serving intention, that change could contribute more to meeting corporate social responsibilities than a whole new maze of government red tape and regulation. If one engineer were to make it a heartfelt intention to place the long-run well-being of the consumer above short-run profits, that change in intention could have more impact on the design of products than a multimillion-dollar safety study funded by the federal government. If one media executive were to view his or her task as that of promoting the active social learning of a culture rather than maximizing short-run profits from mindless, consumer-oriented programming, that change could have more impact than a thousand letters and petitions from despairing viewers.

The point is that we all have our unique work to do and our unique contributions to make to life. If each person were to begin to act in a more compassionate manner, no matter how imperfect or tentative his or her actions, the cumulative result for the entire society would be enormous. Bit by bit, small changes would accumulate into a tidal wave of revitalizing change.

Three foundations for global relations have been considered: force, law, and compassion (or love). We may imagine love to be quite utopian, but consider the alternatives. In not choosing love we are left with law and the prospect of global bureaucratic stagnation. In not choosing law we are left with force and the prospect of either global devastation or global domination. If we value our freedom and vitality as a species, we are obliged to do no less than learn to love one another as a human family or else destroy ourselves in the learning.

POSITIVE VISIONS OF A SUSTAINABLE
FUTURE

The Bible says, "Where there is no vision, the people perish." This seems particularly true as we move into an unprecedented time in human affairs where entirely new approaches to living are needed if we are to build a sustainable future. Many people can visualize a future of worsening crisis—ecological destruction, widespread famine, civil unrest, and material limitation—but few have a positive vision of the future. Without a hopeful future to work toward, people will tend to withdraw into a protected world for themselves and focus on the short run, thereby setting into motion a self-fulfilling pattern of expectation and behavior. We need to see that, with new patterns of consumption, new modes of housing and community, new types of livelihood, and so on, we can create a sustainable *and* a satisfying future.

We cannot consciously build a future we cannot imagine. A first requirement, then, is to create for ourselves a realistic, compelling, and engaging vision of the future that can be simply told. If our collective visualization of the future is weak and fragmented, then our capacity to create a future together will be commensurately diminished. Without a strong sense of the future and a meaningful orientation for our lives, we can lose confidence in ourselves, our leaders, and our institutions. A disoriented world civilization is a recipe for social anarchy or religious fanaticism or authoritarian domination.

Currently the world is drifting along without a compelling and convincing image of the future. We need to discover the story that summarizes the next stage in our evolutionary agenda and works as a catalyst for our energy and enthusiasm. We need to know that living is more than only not dying, that we are going somewhere as a species, that we are doing more than simply maintaining ourselves, that we are working to surpass ourselves. Although we now have few positive images of the future, we should not be discouraged—this is a measure of our freedom to creatively envision new possibilities for humanity.

CONCLUSION

Just as the individual expression of voluntary simplicity is to be found in the intention of living with balance, so, too, with its social expression. A revitalizing civilization will be characterized by greater balance between material excess and material impoverishment, between huge cities and small communities, between massive corporations and smaller companies, between highly specialized work roles and more generalized work roles, and so on. The challenge is to apply our compassion, ingenuity, and tolerance in finding a middle path through life.

A revitalizing civilization that is founded upon a way of life of conscious simplicity offers no magical cure-alls for our planet's ills. The problems generated by the past two centuries of industrialization cannot be suddenly erased. Our challenge is to rise to the occasion and begin, in earnest, the process of revitalizing our faltering industrial civilizations.

Industrialized nations have entered a transitional time. An enormous distance has been traveled over the past several hundred years—social, psychological, technical, and political. We have entered a new situation in human affairs. We are like adolescents who face the irreversible fact of aging and the unavoidable necessity of assuming the difficult responsibilities of adulthood. We are confronted with the challenge of moving beyond our civilizational adolescence and into a new stage of maturity. As we experience the waning of the industrial era and the great uncertainty at having to make our way in a world that seems barely comprehensible, we may feel a great longing for our earlier innocence. Yet it is our responsibility to reestablish our relationship with the world in a manner that holds the prospect of building a sustainable and satisfying future. Whole new dimensions of human opportunity await us if we will rise to the challenge of living more consciously and simply.

Appendix

The Simplicity Survey

The material developed in Chapter 2 was drawn from responses to a questionnaire that appeared in the Summer 1977 issue of *Co-Evolution Quarterly.* This questionnaire, shown below, accompanied the article entitled "Voluntary Simplicity" that was coauthored by Arnold Mitchell.

Name (optional) ____________

Address (optional) ____________

1. Age: ___
2. Sex: Male ☐ Female ☐
3. Married ☐ Single ☐ Living Together ☐
4. Race: White ☐ Black ☐ Brown ☐ Other ____________
5. Personal Annual Income:
   - Under $3,000 ☐
   - $3,000–$5,000 ☐
   - $5,000–$8,000 ☐
   - $8,000–$12,000 ☐
   - $12,000–$16,000 ☐
   - $16,000–$25,000 ☐
   - Over $25,000 ☐
6. Education:
   - No high school diploma ☐
   - High school graduate ☐
   - Some college ☐
   - College graduate ☐
   - Some postgraduate schooling ☐
   - M.A. or M.S. or equivalent ☐

Ph.D., L.L.D., M.D., or equivalent ☐

7. Politics:
Democrat ☐
Republican ☐
Independent ☐
Other _____

8. Place of Residence:
☐ Rural (country)
☐ Small rural town (under 10,000)
☐ Suburban town (under 100,000)
☐ Small city (100,000–500,000)
☐ Big city (over 500,000)

9. Would you characterize your family during your childhood and adolescent years as being:
☐ low income
☐ middle income
☐ high income?
(High would be today's equivalent of $25,000 or more; low would be today's equivalent of $5,000 or less.)

10. Are you now practicing or actively involved with a particular inner-growth process? (Check those that apply)
☐ Traditional religion (e.g., Catholicism, Judaism, Christianity)

☐ Meditative discipline (e.g., TM, Zen, yoga)
☐ Psychotherapy (e.g., Freudian, Jungian, Behaviorist)
☐ Human Potential (e.g., encounter, gestalt, psychosynthesis, Rolfing)
☐ Other (e.g., biofeedback, hypnosis, mind-expanding drugs)

11. To what extent do you feel supported by friends and larger community in pursuit of your inner-growth processes?
☐ Discouraged
☐ Tolerated (neither encouraged nor discouraged)
☐ Some support
☐ A great deal of support

12. Would you describe yourself today as living a life of:
☐ "full" voluntary simplicity
☐ "partial" voluntary simplicity
☐ sympathetic only
☐ indifferent to it
☐ opposed to it
☐ unaware of it

13. If you are fully living the VS style, could you please help us understand what this means by commenting on the questions below:

 a. At what age and under what circumstances did you consciously start to live simply?

 b. Why did you take up voluntary simplicity?

 c. What are the major changes in living arrangements you made as a result?

 d. Please comment on the satisfactions and dissatisfactions associated with this way of life.

 e. Do you see it as a movement that is likely to spread rapidly? Why or why not?

14. If you rate yourself as a "partial" adherent to voluntary simplicity:

 a. In what ways are you acting in VS style?

 b. In what ways are you not acting in VS style?

 c. Do you expect to become ☐ more so, ☐ less so, or ☐ remain the same for the foreseeable future? Why?

 d. What kinds of things would prompt you to embrace more fully a lifestyle of voluntary simplicity?

15. If you are sympathetic to VS but not acting substantially on your sympathy, could you say why you are not and what might trigger you to change your lifestyle in the direction of VS?

16. If you are opposed to voluntary simplicity, could you give us your main reasons why?

17. Did you disagree with parts of this article? If so, what parts?

18. Do you think we omitted important points?

Thanks tremendously for your help.

Duane S. Elgin
Arnold Mitchell

NOTES

CHAPTER ONE: VOLUNTARY SIMPLICITY AND THE NEW GLOBAL CHALLENGE

[1] Richard Gregg, "Voluntary Simplicity," reprinted in *Co-Evolution Quarterly,* Sausalito, Calif., Summer 1977 (originally published in the Indian journal *Visva-Bharati Quarterly* in August 1936).

[2] Donella H. Meadows, et. al., *Beyond the Limits* (Post Mills, Vt.: Chelsea Green Publishing, 1992), p. 196.

[3] Arnold Toynbee, *A Study of History,* Vol. 1 (New York: Oxford University Press, 1947), p. 198.

[4] David Shi, *The Simple Life: Plain Living and High Thinking in American Culture* (New York: Oxford University Press, 1985), p. 145.

[5] Ibid., p. 187.

[6] Gregg, op. cit, p. 20.

[7] Shi, op. cit, p. 149.

[8] Quoted in Gregg, op. cit, p. 27.

[9] Results from the 1992 *Human Development Report* (published

by the United Nations) were reported in the *San Francisco Chronicle*, April 24, 1992, p. 20.

[10] This definition of absolute poverty was taken from the "Address to the Board of Governors" of the World Bank by Robert McNamara, president, September 30, 1980, Washington, D.C.

[11] See, for example, George Sanderson, "Climate Change: The Threat to Human Health," in *The Futurist*, Bethesda, Md., March–April 1992.

[12] Ibid.

[13] Survey done by *Research & Forecasts* for Chivas Regal, reported in the article by Ronald Henkoff, "Is Greed Dead," *Fortune*, August 14, 1989. Regional polls confirm these findings. A poll conducted in the San Francisco Bay area in 1986 found that when people were "given a choice between a simpler life with fewer material possessions and reaching a higher standard of living, they favored the simpler life by almost 3 to 1." Reported in the *San Francisco Chronicle*, October 2, 1986.

[14] David Shi's book, *The Simple Life,* was invaluable in developing this historical overview.

[15] Doris Janzen Longacre, *Living More with Less* (Scottdale, Pa.: Herald Press, 1980), p. 13.

[16] Adam Finnerty, *No More Plastic Jesus* (New York: Orbis Books, 1977).

[17] Quoted in Goldian VandenBroek, ed., *Less Is More* (New York: Harper Colophon Books, 1978), p. 116.

[18] Ibid, p. 60.

[19] Walpola Rahula, "The Social Teachings of the Buddha," in Fred Eppsteiner, ed., *The Path of Compassion,* 2nd ed. (Berkeley, Calif.: Parallax Press, 1988), pp. 103–110.

[20] Sulak Sivaraksa, "Buddhism in a World of Change," Eppsteiner, op. cit., p. 17.

[21] E. F. Schumacher, *Small Is Beautiful* (London: Blond & Briggs, 1973), p. 52.

[22] Shi, op. cit, p. 4.

23 Ibid., p. 127.

24 Shi, Ibid., pp. 3–4.

CHAPTER TWO: PEOPLE LIVING THE SIMPLE LIFE

1 This statement of Greenpeace philosophy was taken from their literature (Greenpeace, Fort Mason, San Francisco, Calif. 94123).

2 Ibid.

3 E. F. Schumacher, "Taking the Scare Out of Scarcity," *Psychology Today*, September 1977, p. 16.

CHAPTER THREE: APPRECIATING LIFE

1 Quoted in Lincoln Barnett, *The Universe and Dr. Einstein* (New York: Bantam Books, 1957), p. 108.

2 Bill Broder, *The Sacred Hoop* (San Francisco: Sierra Club Books, 1979).

3 Kenneth Ring, *Life at Death: A Scientific Investigation of the Near-Death Experience* (New York: Quill, 1982), pp. 141–143.

4 Ibid., p. 141.

5 Ibid., p. 143.

6 Quoted in Thomas Merton, *Gandhi on Non-Violence* (New York: New Directions Publishing, 1965), p. 68.

7 Quoted in Ram Dass, *Journey of Awakening* (New York: Bantam Books, 1978), p. 5.

8 L. W. Yaggy and T. L. Haines, *The Royal Path of Life* (Chicago: Western Publishing House, 1877), p. 590.

CHAPTER FOUR: LIVING MORE
VOLUNTARILY

[1] Roger Walsh, "Initial Meditative Experiences: Part I," *Journal of Transpersonal Psychology,* No. 2 (1977) p. 154.

[2] E. F. Schumacher, *A Guide for the Perplexed* (New York: Harper & Row, 1977), p. 119.

[3] See, for example: Arthur Deikman, *Personal Freedom* (New York: Viking Press, 1976); Chogyam Trungpa, "Foundations of Mindfulness," in *Garuda IV* (Berkeley, Calif.: Shambala Press, 1976); Sri Nisargadatta Maharaj, *I Am That,* Vols. I and II, Maurice Frydman (trans.) (Bombay, India: Chetana, 1973); Joseph Goldstein, *The Experience of Insight* (Santa Cruz, Calif.: Unity Press, 1976); Satprem, *Sri Aurobindo or the Adventure of Consciousness* (New York: Harper & Row, 1968).

[4] See, for example, Aldous Huxley, *The Perennial Philosophy* (New York: Harper, 1945); Huston Smith, *The Religions of Mankind* (New York: Harper & Row, 1958).

[5] Paul Tillich, *Love, Power and Justice* (New York: Oxford University Press, 1954).

CHAPTER FIVE: LIVING MORE SIMPLY

[1] I am grateful to Arnold Mitchell for suggesting this illuminating example.

[2] These questions were taken from an early version of the book *Taking Charge,* which was written by the Simple Living Collective of San Francisco; published in New York by Bantam Books, 1977.

[3] *The Spiritual Teaching of Ramana Maharshi* (Berkeley, Calif.: Shambala Press, 1972), p. 56.

[4] James Prescott, "Body Pleasure and the Origins of Violence," *Bulletin of Atomic Scientists,* November 1975.

CHAPTER SIX: CIVILIZATIONS IN TRANSITION

[1] Arnold Toynbee, *A Study of History* (Great Britain: Weathervane Books/Oxford University Press, 1972), p. 137.

CHAPTER SEVEN: CIVILIZATIONAL REVITALIZATION

[1] George Gallup, "50 Years of American Opinion," *San Francisco Chronicle,* October 21, 1985.

[2] Quoted in Eknath Easwaran, *Gandhi the Man* (Petaluma, Calif.: Nilgiri Press, 1978), p. 56.

Suggested Readings

Joe Dominguez and Vicki Robin, *Your Money or Your Life* (New York: Viking Press, 1992). A cornucopia of insight—financial, practical, emotional, and spiritual—about transforming your relationship with money and achieving financial independence. Energized with the personal stories of real people, this book describes an inspiring path for living with frugality, integrity, and compassion.

Alan Durning, *How Much Is Enough?: The Consumer Society and the Future of the Earth* (New York: W. W. Norton, 1992). Explores the impact of the consumer revolution on human happiness and the environment. Then considers what levels of consumption are sufficient to meet our needs and how we can foster a "culture of permanence."

Lester W. Milbrath, *Envisioning a Sustainable Society: Learning Our Way Out* (Albany, N.Y.: State University of New York Press, 1989). An in-depth exploration of why modern, consumerist societies are not sustainable. Followed by a vision of a sustainable society and how to make the transition to it.

Albert Gore, *Earth in the Balance: Ecology and the Human Spirit* (New York: Houghton Mifflin, 1992). Describes the global environmental crisis and the national and global initiatives that need to be made if the human family is to restore its balance with nature.

Donella Meadows, et. al., *Beyond the Limits: Confronting Global Collapse, Envisioning a Sustainable Future* (Post Mills,Vt.: Chelsea Green Publishing, 1992). An updated version of the landmark book *Limits to Growth*, which was published twenty years earlier. Develops computer projections of various scenarios for world growth and shows how current trends are unsustainable. The authors then discuss the transition to a sustainable world system.

Adam Daniel Finnerty, *No More Plastic Jesus: Global Justice and Christian Lifestyle* (Maryknoll, N.Y.: Orbis Books, 1977). Explores issues of overconsumption, pollution, and the just uses of the world's resources from a Christian perspective. Finnerty describes how Christians can translate their religious perspectives into new lifestyle choices.

Ronald S. Miller, *As Above So Below: Paths to Spiritual Renewal in Daily Life* (Los Angeles: Jeremy Tarcher, Inc., 1992). A rich exploration of the "new spirituality and its diversity of expressions; for example, Western and Eastern wisdom traditions, healing, art, dreamwork, mythology, compassionate action, and much more.

Thich Nhat Hanh, *Peace Is Every Step: The Path of Mindfulness in Everyday Life* (New York: Bantam Books, 1991). A book of personal stories, meditations, and commentaries drawn from his experience as a peace activist, teacher, and community leader. With great compassion he shows how to bring the meditation process into everyday activities such as walking, driving a car, cooking, and working.

Ram Dass, *Journey of Awakening: A Meditator's Guidebook* (New York: Bantam Books, 1990)—second edition. Ram

Dass describes various spiritual practices and offers advice on how to find a meditative path appropriate for oneself. Topics include: getting your bearings, picking a path, finding your way, losing your way, and many more.

Linda Marks, *Living with Vision: Reclaiming the Power of the Heart* (Indianapolis: Knowledge Systems, Inc., 1989). A book about discovering, and living out, one's personal vision and sense of life purpose. It is filled with exercises and insights for developing a way of life that is in harmony with nature and the universe.

Goldian VandenBroeck, editor, *Less Is More: The Art of Voluntary Poverty* (New York: Harper Colophon Books, 1978). A treasury of quotations from around the world and throughout history regarding the nature and value of the simple life.

David Shi, *The Simple Life: Plain Living and High Thinking in American Culture* (New York: Oxford University Press, 1985). An in-depth exploration of the history of the simple life in the United States—from the Puritans and Quakers to the Transcendentalists and Progressives, and beyond.

Adbusters Quarterly, published by the Media Foundation (1243 West 7th Ave., Vancouver, B.C., V6H 1B7 Canada). A lively magazine that challenges television advertising in particular and the consumerist mind-set of industrial cultures in general. The Media Foundation also helps people produce and air their own countercommercials intended to foster ecological ways of living.

AdVice, newsletter of the Center for the Study of Commercialism (1875 Connecticut Ave., N.W., Suite 300, Washington, D.C. 20009-5728). The center researches, publicizes, and opposes the invasion of commercialism into nearly every facet of life in developed nations, particularly the United States.

INDEX

alienation, 145
  work and, 101, 156
Aquinas, Thomas, 156
Aristotle, 50
authoritarianism, 178

balance, 25, 157, 217
  consumption patterns
    and, 28, 147–149
  between external technol-
    ogies and inner learn-
    ing, 138–139
  of feminine-masculine
    qualities, 97–98
  global interdependence
    and, 42–43, 48,
    183–184
  between maintaining our-
    selves and surpassing
    ourselves, 36–37,
    183
  in pleasure-pain contin-
    uum, 107–108

Basil the Great, 47–48
blame, responsibility vs.,
    172–174
Boulding, Elise, 59
Buber, Martin, 83
bureaucracy:
  grass roots organizations
    vs., 181
  in highly managed social
    order, 181, 184–
    185
  as inimical "workplace,"
    156
  legalistic foundations and,
    212
  paternalistic, 184

change:
  "human nature" and,
    139–141
  opportunities for, 43–46,
    192–194
  pathways of, 71–77

change (*cont.*)
  psychological stress and, 74, 164
  revitalization as, *see* revitalization of civilization
  small, cumulative effect of, 58, 59–60, 73–74, 109, 215
  stages-of-growth model and, 164–171
  in tax structure, 198–199
  by VS proponents, 27–39, 73–74, 108–110
civilization:
  challenge of Stage IV for, 176–178
  characteristics of Breakdown Stage for, 176
  creativity and, 167–168, 170, 173, 181, 184
  critical global problems and, 36–44, 171–172, 218
  four-stage model of, 164–171
  future alternatives for, 178–191, 216–217
  as global, 42–43, 186–192, 209–215
  responsibility vs. blame in decline of, 172–174
  revitalization of, *see* revitalization of civilization
  Stage I of (High Growth), 166, 167
  Stage II of (Full Blossoming), 166, 167–168
  Stage III of (Initial Decline), 166, 168–169
  Stage IV of (Breakdown), 166, 170–171
  stages-of-growth model for, 164–171, 174–175
  in transition, 163–194
  transition dynamics in, 178–190, 192–194, 218
  true, 49
  United States as Stage IV example of, 171
  VS's contribution to, 28, 110
Co-Evolution Quarterly, 60
common sense:
  in challenge of Breakdown Stage, 176–177
  global civilization as, 190–191
communication, interpersonal, 35, 153–155
communication rights movement, 209
community, 32, 34–35, 54, 87–89, 200–201
compassion:
  in approach to life, 35, 46–47, 157–158
  consumption patterns and, 101–102, 148–149
  as foundation for global community, 211, 217–218
consciously living, 123–124, 128–142
  creativity and, 137–138
  ecological orientation and, 138–139

enabling qualities of, 136–142, 212–213
"human nature" and, 139–141
as "life-sensing," 157–160
relationships and, 128–129, 136–139
self-remembering and, 128–133
consciousness:
as compassionate intention, 59–60
embedded, 131–133
meaning of, 128
"new," 24
self-reflective, 131–133, 136–142
consumption patterns:
of basic foods, 34
high, male dominance and, 97
identity and, 149–150
mass media as influence on, 201–206
needs vs. wants in, 147
VS and, 28, 33–34, 147–152
contributory livelihood, VS and, 34, 98–102, 151–152, 155–156
creativity:
in adaptation to future, 137–138, 181
bureaucracy vs., 212
civilizational decline and, 167–168, 170, 173, 182
grass roots organizations and, 181

daily living, 108–110
experiences of VS in, 71–77
death, as ally, 117–121, 146
de Beauvoir, Simone, 36
decentralization process, 188, 198
democratic processes:
law and, 211–212
stagnation and, 181, 184–185
television and, 187–188, 189, 207–209
despair, Breakdown Stage and, 170, 176
developing nations, equitable sharing with, 42–43, 48, 183–184

Eastern philosophy/psychology, 48–50, 79–80, 127, 134–135, 213–214
ecological perspectives:
consumption patterns and, 151–152
Greenpeace Movement and, 93
of VS supporters, 92–94, 138–139, 197–201
economy:
democratization of, 157, 198–199
personal autonomy and, 101–102
VS and, 28, 197–201
Einstein, Albert, 115
electronic town meetings, 208–209
Emerson, Ralph Waldo, 52–53

entrepreneurship, 101–102, 198
environments, living and working, 34–35, 156
in revitalizing society, 115

feminism:
as liberating, 94–98
as model for cultural alternatives, 96–97
Fortune, 44–45
future, alternate scenarios for, 178–194, 216–217
futures research, 60

Gandhi, Mohandas K., 32, 48–49, 118, 211
global civilization, as future course, 42–43, 186–194, 209–215
"golden rule," 47–53, 215
grass roots organizations, 181, 188, 189
grass roots VS survey, 60–109
conclusions drawn from, 62–63, 108–110
daily life changes reported in, 71–77
definitions emerging from, 63–66
demographic background of, 61–62, 80
feminist concerns reported in, 94–98
inner-growth component in, 77–83
motivations for change given in, 67–70
policies reflected in, 89–94
relationships discussed in, 83–87
satisfactions and dissatisfactions revealed in, 102–108
work backgrounds found in, 98–100
Greeks, early, 50
Greenpeace Movement, 93
Gregg, Richard, 23, 31
growth, four-stage model of, 164–171

"human nature," 139–141

identity, consumption and, 149–150
Indians, American, 115
individual:
control and power of, 34–35, 60, 91–92, 106–108, 109–110, 124–125, 149–150, 192–194
cumulative impact of, 59–60
dignity of, 90
diversity of VS forms for, 31, 32, 65, 80–81
personal VS experiences of, 60–109
responsibility by, 53–55, 106, 156, 174, 192–194, 218
industrial era:
critical global problems in, 36–44, 171–172, 218
growth model for, 164–171
in initial decline stage, 163, 175

loss of social cohesion in,
176
"masculinity" and, 97
from planetary perspec-
tive, 190–192
industrial work view,
107
inner-growth process, 81–
83
Eastern contributions to,
79–80
VS and, 36–39, 77–83,
110
"Is Greed Dead?," 44–45

Jesus, teaching of, 46–47,
134

Lao-tzu, teaching of, 48
law, as foundation for
global community,
211–212
"Law of Progressive Simplification" (Toynbee),
195
life:
death as ally of, 117–121,
146
preciousness of, 90
simplicity and, 145–146
VS in context of, 113–
121
lifeboat ethic, 181
love, 110
as practical, 213–214
as unity, 134–135

Maharshi, Ramana, 154
mass media:
in revitalization alternative, 187–188, 189

in stagnation and collapse
alternatives, 180–
181, 185
see also television
meditation, 79–80, 127
Mitchell, Arnold, 60

"near death" experiences,
117–118
neighborhoods, 54
"new consciousness," 24
new frontier concept, 60–
109
nonviolent activism, 93–
94

"Perennial Philosophy,"
134–135
Picasso, Pablo, 30
Plato, 50
politics:
law and, 211–212
local- and global-level
vs. national-level,
92–94
in stagnating civilization,
181, 184–185
of VS, 89–94, 109–110
poverty, simplicity vs., 26–
28, 40, 143–144
problems, critical, 36–44,
171–172, 218
Puritans, 30, 50–51

Quakers, 51–52

relationships, 32
communications in, 35,
153–155
conscious living and, 83–
87, 128–129, 136

religions, traditional, 46–
48, 80–81, 83, 134–
135, 213–214
revitalization of civilization,
178, 186–190
characteristics of, 217–
218
enabling qualities for,
136–142, 212–213
grass roots organizations
and, 181
life-sensing and life-serving orientation in,
157–159
mass media and, 187–
188, 189
VS and, 195–218
see also social evolution
Ring, Kenneth, 117–118
role models, 35, 94–98
television and, 203

scale, 44
human-sized, 34–35, 156
Schumacher, E. F., 49–50,
106–107, 127–128
self-determination, 34, 91–
92, 106–108, 124–
125, 192–194
self-realization, 124–125,
149–150
sexual stereotypes, 35, 94–
95, 96–98
"Shakertown Pledge," 48
Shi, David, 53
"Simple Life, The," 44
simplicity:
aesthetic nature of, 30–
31, 48, 150
as consciously chosen,
24–25, 143–144

as enabling, 27, 45, 149
poverty vs., 26–28, 143–
144
as progressive movement,
31
reasons for, 24–25
simplicity in living, 143–160
balance in, 36–37, 46,
147–149, 156, 157
consumption and, 147–
152
interpersonal communica-
tions and, 35, 153–
155
meaning of, 145, 157–
158
as voluntary, 27–28,
143–144
work and, 34–35, 98–
102, 155–157
Sivaraska, Sulak, 49
Small Is Beautiful (Schu-
macher), 49–50
"small is beautiful" concept,
49–50, 109
social evolution, 211
conscious living in, 138–
142
social learning, 181, 187–
188
television's default in,
181, 187–188
social order, global scenarios for:
highly managed, 181,
184–185
love in, 212–213
see also civilization
social reality, conscious living and, 136–139
see also reality

social systems, authoritarian outcomes in, 178
Socrates, 50
spiritual life, 77–83
stagnation and collapse of civilization, 178, 179–186
  mass media and, 180–181, 185
  psychological responses and, 179–181
  retreat to highly managed social order in, 181, 184–185
Stair, Nadine, 118–119
Stanford Research Institute (SRI International), 60

tax structure, changes in, 198–199
technical problems (energy and resources), 33–35, 37–44, 138–139, 171–172
television:
  conspicuous consumption and, 202–204
  public interest ignored by, 180–181
  social learning and, 181, 187–188
  transformation of, 187–188, 189, 201–206, 207–209
Thoreau, Henry David, 31, 52–53
Tillich, Paul, 135
Time, 44
town meetings, electronic, 208–209

Toynbee, Arnold, 165, 173–174, 195
Transcendentalism, 52–53

United Nations Human Development Report (1992), 42
United States, 171
universe:
  holistic view of, 114
  as "our home," 114–116, 146

values, mainstream, 38–39, 88
  in growth model, 166–170
voluntary living, 123–142
  consciousness in, *see* consciously living
  explained, 23–25, 123–124
  "running on automatic" vs., 124–125
  social implications of, 127–139
Voluntary Simplicity (VS):
  attitudes in, 38–39, 77–83, 108–110
  "back to the land" movement vs., 30, 110
  basic ideas in, 23–25
  as consciously chosen, 144
  as crucial to progress, 28
  definitions of, 23–25, 48, 63–66
  as evolutionary process, 73–74
  faddishness rejected by, 36–37, 65–66

Voluntary Simplicity (*cont.*)
grass roots survey on,
60–109
individual design of, 31,
32, 65, 80–81, 109
industrial era view vs.,
38–39, 109–110
as integrated path, 108,
110, 157–160
participation vs. isolation
in, 30, 109–110
paths found to, 71–77,
80–81
politics of, 89–94, 109–
110
present as initial stage in,
108
reasons for choosing, 67–
70
relevance for civilizational
transition, 28
relevance of death to,
117–121

satisfactions and dissatisfactions of, 102–108
supporters of, as "pi-
oneers," 109, 110
universe as context for,
114–116
worldly expressions of,
32–35

Walsh, Roger, 125–127
Wright, Frank Lloyd, 30–
31
work:
contributory livelihood
and, 34, 98–102,
151–152, 155–156
direct worker participa-
tion in, 101, 157,
198
human-sized places of,
34–35, 156
as life-serving, 101–102
simplicity and, 155–157